Whitewater and Sea

KAYAKING

OUTDOOR PURSUITS SERIES

Kent Ford

Human Kinetics

Library of Congress Cataloging-in-Publication Data

Ford, Kent, 1957-
    Kayaking / Kent Ford.
      p.   cm. -- (Outdoor pursuits series)
    Includes index.
    ISBN 0-87322-688-7 (pbk.)
    1. Kayaking. I. Title. II. Series.
    GV783.F75   1995
    797.1'224--dc20
                                               95-2207
                                             CIP

ISBN: 0-87322-688-7

Series Editor and Developmental Editor: Holly Gilly; **Assistant Editors:** Kirby Mittelmeier, Elaine Crabtree; **Copyeditor:** Karen Bojda; **Proofreader:** Jim Burns; **Photo Editor:** Boyd LaFoon; **Typesetter:** Ruby Zimmerman; **Text Designer:** Keith Blomberg; **Layout Artist:** Stuart Cartwright; **Cover Designer:** Jack Davis; **Cover and Principle Interior Photography:** Wiley/Wales; **Illustrator:** Thomas • Bradley

Photos on pages 54 and 55 by Chris Brown.

Human Kinetics books are available at special discounts for bulk purchase. Special editions or book excerpts can also be created to specification. For details, contact the Special Sales Manager at Human Kinetics.

Printed in Hong Kong   10 9 8 7 6 5 4 3 2 1

Human Kinetics
P.O. Box 5076, Champaign, IL 61825-5076
1-800-747-4457

Canada: Human Kinetics, Box 24040, Windsor, ON N8Y 4Y9
1-800-465-7301 (in Canada only)

Europe: Human Kinetics, P.O. Box IW14, Leeds LS16 6TR, England
(44) 532 781708

Australia: Human Kinetics, 2 Ingrid Street, Clapham 5062, South Australia
(08) 371 3755

New Zealand: Human Kinetics, P.O. Box 105-231, Auckland 1
(09) 309 2259

CONTENTS

Note: Kayaking is potentially dangerous. This book can help you understand how to have fun in the sport safely; however, it is not intended to replace on-the-water instruction, which is highly recommended.

1

GOING
KAYAKING

It's going to be a beautiful, scorching hot summer weekend. There's nowhere I'd rather be than on the water. Where should I go for some fun?

Maybe I'll head to the local whitewater run. It's a bouncy Class II–III whitewater, with enough rocks to give it a playful character. I can imagine my boat gliding along through some chop before I power around a rock, carve through an eddy, and peel out into some bigger, rolling waves. I catch another eddy and join some friends at the best surf wave on the river. We take turns on the wave, hooting with delight when a friend gets blasted in the face by a wave or when we catch a long ride. By the end of the day we're starving, pleasantly exhausted, and longing for dry clothes. This beats sitting around on a hot day!

Or I could head out in my sea kayak. Some friends know a set of islands with spectacular marine life just off the coast. If we're lucky, we'll see some dolphins that will come to play with us as we cruise around the island. We'll try to find the sea caves described in our last club newsletter. The caves and cliffs have exquisitely sculpted rock formations, polished by big seas, and a colorful treat of varied rocks and lichens. We should get some good exercise combined with a relaxing day of nature watching.

Sea kayaking and whitewater kayaking are different in many ways, yet equally satisfying. Kayaking has become a love affair for me as I've learned to tap into the energy and become as fluid as the water. Kayaking has become a passion of tranquillity as well as thrills.

This book is designed to acquaint you with the joys of kayaking. I'll help you figure out what sort of kayaking you may be interested in, then I'll give you hints on how to choose the equipment and apparel you'll need to be comfortable and safe. I'll explain some of the details of kayak strokes so that you can move the boat on the water to where you want to go. It's essential

Whitewater can offer thrills.

that you know how to kayak safely on the ocean and coastlines as well as on whitewater, so I devote a chapter each to whitewater and sea kayaking techniques and safety. I also describe some of the very best places in the world to kayak, and I tell you about other paddle-sport activities you might like if you find that you've become hooked on kayaking. My goal is to help you learn to enjoy the sport safely and comfortably.

Keep in mind that learning to kayak is a process, not a destination. Even as you become very proficient in the sport, you will be constantly learning to improve your technique and your ability to enjoy the water.

What's Your Pleasure?

Deciding whether you want to explore whitewater kayaking or sea kayaking depends on your personality, the nature of the water in your region, and the type of paddler you want to be. Inevitably, the friends who started you in the

Sea kayaking gets you to some remarkable places.

activity and the people you meet on the water shape the sort of kayaker you become.

The popular image of whitewater kayaking is of risk takers plunging down steep waterfalls, running extremely rock-laced, difficult whitewater. Such scenes are only a small subset of the sport. Most recreational paddlers enjoy looking for quietly rippled water that enables them to play by surfing little waves and to explore some wild and remote places. Sea kayaking offers a similar variety. There is a broad spectrum of paddlers, some of them taking extended trips in fairly remote and difficult waters, others enjoying very light day trips. A realtor friend of mine gets out to paddle at lunch nearly every day of the summer. In the Seattle area, many people commute to work by boat.

Most kayaking is done in solo boats, but in sea kayaking perhaps 20 percent of the kayaks are doubles boats. On the other hand, whitewater kayaking is primarily an individual sport. There are tandem whitewater kayaks, but they are rarely seen.

One of the benefits of kayaking is the full range of ways you can enjoy the activity, from leisurely part-day trips to full expeditions on difficult waters. The virtue of kayaking is that it offers enjoyment to people of all ages and abilities with very different needs.

DETERMINE YOUR KAYAKING PREFERENCE

What's your preference? Some sea kayakers live closer to rivers than the sea, and some whitewater paddlers enjoy the wilderness getaway potential of the sport. Nonetheless, these are the typical traits of each group.

Sea kayaking is for you if . . .

you live near a lake, flatwater river, or ocean.

you want the easy option of self-support camping.

you want a small group or solo getaway.

access to nature and wilderness destinations is your primary motivator.

Whitewater kayaking is for you if . . .

you live near whitewater rivers.

the thrill of outdoor gravity sports is appealing.

you are willing to invest extra time learning.

you don't mind being under water.

sport and physical challenge is your primary motivator.

Kayaking strokes you learn in this book can be applied to sea kayaking or whitewater kayaking. Most of the paddling skills are interchangeable. Depending on the water that's most accessible to you, you can enjoy one style of kayaking near home and the other during vacations.

Learning the basic kayaking maneuvers will help you enjoy a variety of general recreational activities, from fishing to bird watching to longer day tours. If you like point-to-point travel, you might want to combine your kayaking skills with camping. Self-support trips provide an enjoyable way to experience outdoor overnight trips without having to carry a backpack. The boat carries the weight of your gear; all you need to do is pull it up on shore.

The most popular type of whitewater paddling is play paddling. Paddlers use the river's currents, waves, and holes to maneuver, surf, and play. Play paddling tends to be a very safe outlet for the whitewater enthusiast. You can pick rivers and rapids that are commensurate with your ability.

Increasing your skills increases the fun you can have in a kayak.

Basic principles, strokes, and maneuvers are the common thread between all paddle sports. They provide you with the foundation to become a solid multidisciplined paddler and explore other paddle sports. Although the focus in this book is on general recreational kayaking, with further instruction and experience you can modify the basic techniques to suit the demands of any style of kayaking.

Getting Started

You should try the type of kayaking that interests you before you spend a lot of money on equipment. Many opportunities are available for you to experiment without spending a lot of money.

Kayaking Symposia

You can get some short-term exposure to different types of boats at symposia offered by manufacturers and outfitters. They provide the boats and the chance for you to use them in hopes that you'll buy their equipment. Usually you're allowed to test the different kayaks, and you can take advantage of instruction if it's available.

Instructional Schools

Instructional schools provide an ideal way to learn to paddle. They are usually located on easy instructional waterways. Generally, the instructors begin with an orientation. They will introduce you to the equipment and show you how it is used. You should have an opportunity to try different types of equipment during the course. On the water, instructors will teach you how to warm up and how to stroke safely and correctly so you don't develop bad paddling techniques. Schools vary quite a bit in quality, but the best ones give you a solid foundation in the sport and move you up to intermediate level after 3 or 4 days. Paddling schools generally want to make you an independent paddler. This is a pleasant difference from other activities where sometimes an unspoken goal is to get you back for more lessons.

HOW TO CHOOSE A SCHOOL

Get a listing from paddling magazines and ask a friend or a local outfitter's shop to recommend the best. Call the school and ask about their instructors' qualifications:

How long have lead instructors been teaching paddling? (The longer, the better!)

What is the instructor-to-student ratio? (For whitewater, 5:1 should be the maximum; 8:1 in sea kayaking.)

What training do instructors receive? Are they nationally certified? If not, how extensive is in-house training?

What variety of equipment do they have available for rental? (More variety improves your likelihood of finding a good fit and your choice of boats to purchase.)

Are instructors' First Aid and CPR cards current? (The answer better be yes, as this indicates the level of their professionalism.)

Where are lessons conducted? (Look for warm, uncrowded waters appropriate for your skill level.)

Try a regional program for your first time, then perhaps travel to a nationally recognized school for some follow-up. Remember, recommendations are everything!

Paddling Clubs

Another fun way to get involved in kayaking is through a local paddling club. Paddling clubs offer a great way to meet other kayakers, get more education, and hear a little bit about the local rivers and waterways. Some very active whitewater kayaking clubs, such as the one in Manhattan, Kansas, are hundreds of miles from the nearest whitewater river, so don't think that just because you don't live near water you can't kayak.

To find the nearest paddling club, ask at the local outfitter's shop. Check their bulletin board because local paddling clubs and retailers often have a close relationship. Paddling clubs usually have monthly meetings highlighted by interesting speakers who are experienced with the water in your area and around the world. Paddling clubs also offer kayak clinics and trips where it's easy to join with other folks of your ability. The appendix lists a few organizations that can help you find some local expertise.

Join a club to paddle in a group for fun and adventure.

You'll find that paddlers have a lot of passion for kayaking. By joining a paddling club, you'll have a direct link to information about techniques, the latest equipment, and favorite getaways.

Adventure Travel Trips

Taking an adventure travel trip is another way to gain some kayaking experience. Check paddling and outdoor magazines for names of adventure travel companies. The trips vary dramatically in the skill levels and money they require, but several adventure travel companies cater to beginner and intermediate paddlers. Before signing up for a trip, you'll want to check carefully to make sure that your skill matches the level required for the trip.

Before you sign up for a kayak adventure, make sure that the company offers instruction at the beginning of the trip. The tour company should also establish clear group organization on the water and monitor your progress during the day. Many adventure trips last several days and go to more remote locations, requiring greater emphasis on instruction and preparedness.

On Your Way!

I am hooked on kayaking, and I want you to get hooked too, because I'm sure you'll love it once you try it. No matter where you live, kayaking of one sort or another is quite accessible. On a lake or local bay, or on a nearby creek or river, you can really enjoy the water and get to places that very few other people can.

A kayak gets you to places you can access in no other way.

This book will help you learn about how to get started, but it won't substitute for on-the-water instruction. Before packing for your first outing, get solid training from a good instructor. Kayaking can appear so fluid that instruction might seem unnecessary. But the boats like to turn and to turn over. With instruction you quickly learn the simple tricks that keep you on course. I've seen many paddling veterans have difficulties that were corrected after only one day of instruction. Instruction also teaches you to paddle well, which means paddling efficiently and getting good return for the energy expended. Efficient paddling lets you paddle farther and stronger.

After you've decided on the type of kayaking that you want to try, you'll need to get the right equipment. Chapter 2 helps you choose the gear and clothing you need for the type of paddling you want to do.

2

KAYAKING EQUIPMENT

If you look through a kayak buyer's guide to choose a boat and gear, you may discover thousands of different boat designs and more than a hundred varieties of equipment. The number of styles and the subtle differences in form and function can make your head spin. Fortunately, it's easy to narrow down the choices to a selection of gear that is well suited to the recreational paddler.

A Closer Look at Kayaks

Whitewater play boats are fairly short (10–12 ft, 3.0–3.7 m), somewhat broad, and have a blunt entry into the water, characteristics that make sense for spinning and dancing through waves and rapids. Sea kayaks, in contrast, are generally much longer (15–18 ft, 4.6–5.5 m) and have a finer entry into the water. This shape helps them go straight easily. The bottom of the boat, called the hull, affects the tracking and turning characteristics of the boat, while the top of the boat, the deck, keeps the water out and helps the handling in big waves.

Anatomy of a Kayak

Let's look at a few features of the boat a little more closely. Starting at the boat's ends, or bow (front) and stern (back), we find grab loops, or little handles that are part of the rescue towing system. They are necessary for pulling a friend to shore, or for helping you hold onto the boat after a flip and an unintentional swim. On the deck, around the seat area, is the cockpit rim. The elastic cord of the spray skirt fits around the rim, and the skirt tapers to fit around your waist to keep the water out. While you are running rapids or big swells, the spray skirt helps keep water out of the boat.

Inside a whitewater boat is a foam pillar that runs the length of the boat, adding stiffness to the deck and flotation to the boat. Flotation bags filled with air fit on either side of the foam wall to provide extra flotation in the event of a swim. The boat has a small amount of storage space so you can bring along lunch, a throw rope for rescue, or other small items.

A sea kayak, or touring kayak as it is sometimes called, is often rigged with different accessories designed for the convenience of carrying gear on

A sea kayak has space for a lot of gear for extended trips.

Parts of a Kayak

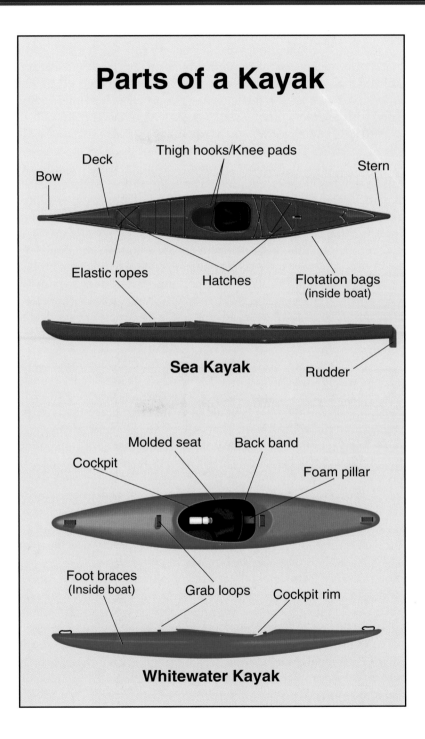

Thigh hooks/Knee pads

Deck

Bow

Stern

Elastic ropes

Hatches

Flotation bags
(inside boat)

Sea Kayak

Rudder

Molded seat Back band

Cockpit

Foam pillar

Foot braces
(Inside boat) Grab loops Cockpit rim

Whitewater Kayak

extended trips. Because the sea kayak is more frequently used as a touring boat, it has hatches that allow you easy access to a lunch sack or to spare clothes. These airtight and watertight compartments also provide flotation for the boat in case it flips over. On the sea kayak's deck you'll find elastic ropes to store your rescue devices, navigation chart, or other items. For extended trips paddlers often install a deck-mounted compass.

Both sea kayaks and whitewater kayaks have a molded seat that shouldn't wobble. The seat is placed close to the bottom of the boat for stability and to maximize comfort in the boat. Some boats have a back rest or back band that alleviates back strain and encourages the proper sitting position. A kayak also has foot braces (often called foot pegs) that are usually adjustable, and thigh hooks or knee pads. Check to make sure that these work together well to brace you in the boat for good control and comfort. Foam can easily be glued to the seat and thigh hooks to enhance your fit and comfort.

Sea kayaks typically have foot-operated rudders that help with turning. These are designed to lift up when going onshore or over logs or weeds. Rudders enable a sea kayak to make big, wide turns; a sea kayak has about twice the turning radius of a car. In contrast, whitewater kayaks don't need rudders because they are so short and turn so easily that a single stroke can spin them in a circle.

High-Tech Materials

The type of material the boat is made of is another choice that you'll have to make when purchasing a boat. There are two basic materials that are used in kayaks today: composite and plastic. The plastic is generally a rotomolded plastic, similar to the big plastic trash cans in front of your house or the Tupperware containers in your freezer. The plastic boats are thick and easily scratched, but more importantly, are almost indestructible. Trash cans you've backed over in the driveway generally spring back into shape. The same is true for the plastic recreational kayaks on the market. (But I don't recommend testing this feature!) Because they are durable and inexpensive, your first kayak will probably be a plastic boat.

For sea kayaking, about half the boats available are composite, since there is less risk they will be damaged by rocks. Composite boats are built with several layers of fabric woven of fiberglass, Kevlar, or carbon fiber material. These fabric layers are impregnated with an epoxy or vinylester resin that cures the boat to the shape of the mold. You can identify Kevlar by its yellowish brown color and carbon because it's black. Composite boats are built from two pieces—the hull and the deck—often of a different color. The two halves are joined by a seam. Regardless of which material is used, these composite boats are generically called "fiberglass," or simply "glass," boats. Composite construction allows the manufacturer to mold finer lines in the boat and at the same time offer better abrasion resistance and a stiffer hull than a plastic boat. However, fiberglass boats require a little bit more maintenance, are complicated to fix in the unlikely event you break them, and are more susceptible to UV breakdown, which means that you should keep them in the shade to prolong their life.

Composite boats made with resins require more time to manufacture than plastic boats, and since they are handmade, they can be almost twice as expensive. You can feel the difference in rigidity and stiffness in the water: The boat seems to glide faster and more easily. For sea kayaks, the lighter weight can be particularly appealing. If you want the very best, it will often be a composite boat.

Choosing a Kayak

The most basic variables in boat design are the length and width. All other things being equal, a longer, narrower boat will be faster than a shorter, fatter boat. But the short, fat boat will turn more easily.

Consider the Design Features

Remember from our earlier discussion of kayaks that whitewater play boats are fairly short and broad and have a blunt entry into the water, while sea kayaks are generally much longer and have a finer entry. The sea kayak and the whitewater play boat represent the two extremes of the design spectrum. Using this basic understanding of design, two different sea kayaks or two different whitewater play boats can be compared by eyeballing the length-to-width ratio. Also look at the entry point at the water line at the very front of the boat. Is it sharp and knifelike, or blunt like a spoon? The entry point can help you guess which boat will probably be faster and which will turn more quickly.

Stability is another factor that is very important when evaluating boats. A boat that is wide along its entire length will be more stable than a boat that is wide only for a short span in the middle and narrow at the ends. Judging this is difficult because the width at the water line is the important variable. A boat whose width is above the water line has a different stability than a boat that has a lot of width below the water line. Paddlers have come up with terms describing two types of stability: initial stability and secondary stability.

Initial stability means that when you rock the boat from side to side, the boat feels very secure, like a stable platform. Boats that have a lot of initial stability generally have a very hard chine, or sharp corner on the hull, when viewed in cross section. Boats with hard chines have a lot of initial stability and generally very little secondary stability. As you lean, the boat is stable up to a point, but then suddenly it will pass the point of stability and tip over. Boats that have solid secondary stability tend to have a rounder hull in the cross section. These boats are not quite as stable when you first enter, but are less prone to tipping over even when rolled far up on their sides.

Generally speaking, you'll want extra stability for general recreation and special uses, such as photography. For racing and other sporting types of kayaking, you'll want a narrower, more responsive, but less stable boat.

Rocker is another feature to consider when deciding what kind of kayak you want to buy. Rocker is the degree to which the hull curves up at the ends, like a banana. A boat that has a lot of rocker will spin more easily, while a boat that has little rocker will be faster.

Consider the Intended Use

The obvious question you need to ask yourself before buying a kayak is: Do I want to kayak on whitewater or on flatwater? You'll want a whitewater kayak for the former and a sea kayak for the latter. But there are even more subsets within those two major categories.

There are a variety of specially designed boats for whitewater including creek boats and polo boats. Creek boats are built for running steep waterfalls

Creek boats are designed for extreme paddling.

and creeks. Curiously, the creek boats usually are very good beginner whitewater boats because they are stable, very round, and generally quite forgiving.

Kayak polo boats share the same blunt appearance as creek boats. These boats are intended for the kayaker's version of water polo, played in swimming pools and lakes.

Inflatable kayaks are a cross between a river raft and a kayak. With this stable and forgiving boat, a relatively inexperienced paddler can quickly learn enough to enjoy easy rapids. For this reason they are often used by rafting companies at times of low water or when rafters want a little extra challenge. An added advantage of inflatable kayaks is the small storage space required for a deflated boat.

Squirt boats are very thin, waferlike kayaks with barely enough room for the legs. These fairly short (8 ft, or 2.5 m) boats are designed for doing stunts like cartwheels in the air or *mystery moves* under the water, where the boat moves through whitewater in such a way that it submerges several feet under the surface for sometimes as long as 30 seconds.

Racing boats are fairly specialized. The whitewater slalom boat is 13 feet (4 m) long, fairly thin with sleek lines, and almost always made of fiberglass or Kevlar material. Slalom boats are built for a combination of speed and maneuverability, with a low profile that allows the paddler to sneak under the slalom poles. See chapter 7 for more information on kayak racing.

Downriver racing is done on whitewater with a decked-over kayak. The long and narrow boat is built for sheer speed over a 4–5 mile (6.5–8.0 km) section of river. The challenge is finding the straightest, fastest route through waves and boulder-laced rapids.

Sea kayaking has a variety of specialty boats as well. Most of those boats are a little more demanding to paddle. Surf kayaks, often called wave skis, are a cross between a kayak and a surfboard. This is a pretty specialized type of kayaking, but depending on where you live and the sort of boating you'll be doing, it might be exactly what you want. Be forewarned that surfers are generally pretty territorial, so paddle tactfully in their areas. However, there are some popular surf kayaking regions open to new paddlers.

"Sit-on-top" kayaks are rapidly gaining popularity for use by the casual and occasional paddler on lakes and accessible flatwater shorelines. These boats have the advantage of simplicity (water never gets inside them) and stability (rather than having to do a roll if you flip over, you merely climb back on top of the boat). Some models have on-deck storage designed for scuba gear. Their disadvantage is that they leave you more exposed to the elements. For some flatwater uses they are ideal. The strokes and skills covered in this book are applicable to sit-on-top boats.

Foldboats are literally foldable kayaks that have the advantage of being easy to transport and store when compacted into their duffel storage bags.

Foldboats are a little slower and less durable than other types of kayaks, but are perfect for airplane travel or when storage space is tight.

Most sea kayaks are designed as day and weekend touring boats, with just enough space for light amounts of gear. But some kayaks are designed specifically with more volume to accommodate gear for multiday expeditions.

© Franz Riegel

Tandem kayaks offer a variety of opportunities.

Tandem kayaks are available if you want the option of taking kids along, or paddling with a person who has a physical disability that precludes solo kayaking. Cockpits designed for three are rare, but are available for family expeditions.

A growing segment of the sea kayaking world enjoys the historical aspect of boat evolution and design. The two major design traditions are Aleut (Alaskan) and Inuit (Greenland). These wooden boats are a joy to look at as well as to paddle. Many artisans enjoy the rewards of exchanging design plans and building their own craft.

WHAT KIND OF KAYAK DO YOU NEED?

Whitewater Kayaks ($700–$1,500)*

If your main use is	*Then you'll want*
Typical	Beginner's play boat
Competition	Slalom kayak or downriver kayak
Fringe maneuvers	Squirt boat
Storage and transportation are key	Inflatable kayak
Waterfall jumping	Creek boat
In swimming pools or ponds	Polo boat

Sea Kayaks ($800–$2,500)

If your main use is	*Then you'll want*
Typical	Day touring kayak
In warm climates	Sit-on-top kayak
Multiday trips	Expedition boat
With kids	Tandem boat
Historical fascination	Aleut or Inuit design
Storage and transportation are key	Foldboat

*Prices are in U.S. dollars.

Try Before You Buy

After you've decided what kind of kayak you want, narrow the field down to a few specific models by investigating manufacturer exhibitions, demo days, symposia, and paddle clubs as I suggested in chapter 1. You can also visit a professional school where they have a variety of different boats that you can try during the course of a day or two. Often sea kayaks are available for rental for day outings, but renting whitewater boats is hit-or-miss, because many organizations are concerned about liability if you get hurt. The likelihood of renting is better if you have taken a class from the organization.

Getting the Right Size

When you've settled on the type of boat you want, you'll need to consider how you fit in specific boats. Boats now come in many sizes. In the earlier days of the sport, kayaks were pretty much built for big, muscular guys and often didn't even fit them comfortably. Today, the ergonomics of outfitting is greatly improved, and now there are kayaks specifically designed for smaller people, for children, and for women.

The bucket seat of most kayaks is form-fitted to someone's bottom, and that bottom probably isn't like yours. If the seat has a sufficient forward angle, you should feel that it encourages you to sit up straight rather than slump in the boat. To find a boat that fits, start by finding a comfortable position on the floor to evaluate your flexibility.

ADOPT THE CORRECT KAYAKING POSTURE

The kayak sitting position is not natural for most of us. Try this exercise to learn correct posture.

1. Wearing a comfortable, loose pair of pants, sit on the floor with your feet straight out in front of you.

2. Lift your knees up and out about a foot and a half (46 cm) apart, with your heels touching and your big toes a foot (30 cm) apart.

3. Place your hand on your lower back and make sure that your back is perpendicular to the floor. Your back should be straight, your chin up, and your chest forward.

You should now be in the correct posture for successful kayaking. If this position is uncomfortable for you, it's probably because your hamstrings are tight. Chapter 3 gives you some flexibility exercises to stretch your hamstrings so you'll be comfortable in the boat.

When you go into a shop to try a boat or when you check one out at a kayak symposium, don't just hop in the boat for a couple of seconds to test the fit. You need to try the boat on as you would a pair of shoes. Take your time; sit in the boat for a while to let the nuances be felt. After sitting for 5 or 10 minutes, think about what parts of your body are complaining. Most boats include an adjustable back band to help you maintain correct paddling posture. Check to make sure the foot braces, thigh hooks, and seat work well together. You can easily glue foam to the seat and thigh hooks to improve the fit and comfort.

Buying Used Boats

Buying a used boat can be an affordable option. A good rule of thumb is to look for boats that are in pretty good condition with no major breaks. A boat that is less than 4 or 5 years old ensures a design that's pretty far along in the evolution of the sport. Some of the older designs are less comfortable, so be especially careful that the boat fits you. Like most major capital expenditures, kayaks depreciate nearly 50 percent in the first year. After 5 years, the value of a kayak in good condition rarely drops to less than a third of its original retail price.

Getting the Right PFD

A personal flotation device (PFD) is the most essential part of a kayaker's gear. You'll wear it all the time in or near the water. Fortunately, PFDs are made with comfort in mind, so you'll hardly even notice it. In fact, you'll get so accustomed to it that you'll feel naked without it.

A PFD helps you float easily in the event of a swim. It helps you get back into your boat and provides some insulation as well as padding. A PFD also protects you from abrasion and provides extra warmth on cold days. Many

Checking the fit of a PFD. You shouldn't be able to lift it past your ear.

states require that you always wear a PFD when in a kayak, but even if laws don't require it, you should make it a habit. It just makes good sense to be prepared for capsizing by wearing a vest-style PFD at all times.

When you're starting out, you should wear a PFD that is U.S. Coast Guard approved, since a growing number of places require that certification. A Coast Guard approved Type III PFD costs between $50 and $130. This vest model is the kind usually used by kayakers because its construction provides adequate flotation in rough waters. The PFD consists of flotation foam sewn into a nylon cover. In some models the foam is a broad flat panel, in others the foam is in tubes that run vertically in narrow pockets. Other flotation devices are designed for larger craft and are not appropriate for kayaking.

A properly fitting PFD will feel snug, but will not inhibit your breathing. The best way to test a PFD is in the water, making sure that it stays low and snug around your torso and doesn't ride up. A PFD can be tested on land. After adjusting the side straps, the waist strap, and zipper, try tugging up at the shoulders. You shouldn't be able to lift the shoulders up past the middle of your ear. If you can raise them past the middle of your ear, then you may need a snugger adjustment or a smaller size. Make sure that your PFD fits comfortably over layers of clothing. A wet suit, sweater, and paddling jacket are commonly worn on the water.

I find that in the teaching I do, I'm constantly reminding my students that the responsibility is with them to make sure that their PFD is fitted, adjusted very snugly, and always on.

Picking a Paddle

The second most costly kayaking investment will probably be your paddle. It's amazing how many times I discover a student of mine using what I consider to be a war club instead of a quality paddle. A lightweight yet stiff paddle is the key to having fun kayaking. A well-designed blade pulls and slices easily in the water. It feels like a natural extension of your upper-body movements.

Top-of-the-line paddles range from $200 to $250, while standard versions can cost from $150 to $200. The most inexpensive paddles might cost $50 or $100. These cheap paddles have an aluminum shaft and a plastic blade. While these aluminum-and-plastic models are maintenance-free, they rarely have a solid or stiff feel in the water.

Paddle Materials

Paddles are made of two types of material: wood and synthetics such as plastic or fiberglass. Wood paddles reward you with a delightful feel both in and out of the water. They respond with a softness and warmth in your hands. However, wood paddles require occasional varnishing and sanding. Also, they are more expensive than synthetics.

Synthetic paddles have aluminum or fiberglass shafts. Their blades are usually fiberglass. They have a broad range of quality and cost. The least expensive ones can be unacceptably flexible and weak, while the best synthetic can rival the finest wood paddle.

AT A GLANCE: PADDLES

Material	Advantage	Disadvantage	Cost
wood	delightful feel and aesthetics	occasional maintenance	$150–$250
fiberglass	strength	awkward shaft shape and feel	$150–$200
carbon	lightweight	fragile	$170–$275
plastic	inexpensive	less precise feel	$50–$100

Blade Shape

Blade shape is important to paddle performance. It should allow easy slicing through the water and a secure stroke. Both whitewater and sea kayak paddles typically have a curved blade. The inside of the curved blade is called the power face. Some blades have a convex spoon shape that improves the blade's performance.

Sea kayaking paddles are designed with a narrow, long blade and often have drip rings on the shaft to keep water from dripping on your lap during each stroke. Larger blades are for power, smaller blades are for longer distances. The highest performance blades for flatwater are called wing paddles. Designed for Olympic sprint races, wing paddles have a blade designed for a very efficient forward stroke.

Most kayak paddle blades are offset: when you lay the paddle on the ground, the blades face in different directions. This offset, or blade feathering, makes the paddle easier to use in a head wind and allows for more power on a wide variety of strokes. Today's paddles are offset about 70 degrees. Ten years ago, virtually all paddles were offset 90 degrees. Small and adjustable offsets, which many kayakers believe are easier on the wrist, are becoming more common as the sport evolves.

Sizing a Paddle

To size a paddle, hold it over your head with your arms straight up, at right angles to the shaft. Whitewater kayakers should have a fist width, 4 or 5 inches (10–13 cm), between their hands and the blades. Sea kayakers should hold their hands slightly closer, and have 10 to 20 inches (25–51 cm) between their hands and the blades. The following chart shows the correlation between height and arm span in relation to the paddle length. When shopping for a paddle, expect to find paddles sized in centimeters.

PADDLE SIZES		
Your height and arm span	*Whitewater paddle*	*Sea kayak paddle*
< 5' (< 1.5 m)	190 cm	210 cm
5'– 5'6" (1.5–1.7 m)	196 cm	225 cm
5'6"– 6' (1.7–1.8 m)	204 cm	230 cm
6'–6'6" (1.8–2.0 m)	206 cm	235 cm

Small people should pay attention to the shaft's diameter. Most standard shafts are sized to fit the average male adult's hand size. People with small hands, including most women and children, may want to order special paddles with a smaller blade and shaft diameter. If you experience wrist problems or mild tendinitis from kayaking, your paddle might be the cause.

Sizing a whitewater paddle.

Other Essentials

Nobody needs to be a "gear head" to enjoy kayaking. Only basic equipment is required, and the same gear works well on almost all water. However, the initial investment can be shocking. I recommend top quality equipment for every paddler. If you need to cut corners, do it by buying a used boat. A used boat is easy to sell after a year or two, if you take a real liking to the sport and want to upgrade later.

The Spray Skirt ($60–$100)

The spray skirt fits around your waist and the rim of the boat's cockpit. The skirt's elastic edge seals tightly to the rim, and it tapers to fit around your waist. Generally the inside of the boat stays almost dry when the skirt is in place. Most paddlers use neoprene skirts that fit securely to keep water out effectively. Sea kayaking skirts are sometimes made of nylon, a material well-suited to the boat's large cockpit and the weathering effects of saltwater but not waterproof.

Spray skirts are sized to fit your waist and the boat's cockpit. A skirt's release loop remains in front and on top of the cockpit. A pull releases the skirt for a quick wet exit after a flip. This loop is a kayaker's rip cord. Even without pulling the loop, a spray skirt should not hold you in the boat against your will. Well-supervised and practiced wet exits will give you confidence in your skills and equipment. Read more about this in the next chapter.

Helmet ($40–$100)

Whitewater helmets should fit snugly over your forehead and temples. Test the fit by moving the helmet with your hand: it should slightly move the skin on your forehead, but not be so tight as to be uncomfortable. Stick with helmets designed for whitewater to ensure that they drain water easily. Sea kayakers rarely wear helmets. They wear them only when they are exploring caves or playing around in rocky surf.

Boat Rack ($50–$150)

Once you have a boat you'll need a way to get it to the water. The best way to do this is on top of your vehicle. Rarely are the roof racks that come on a vehicle appropriate for boats, but if your car has rain gutters, it's easy to add a boat rack. Most bike or paddling stores sell racks that fit nicely on a car. When you tie down your boat, do it securely with ropes or webbing straps. A boat flying off a car is a serious hazard to other vehicles and can cause serious damage to your boat and other equipment as well. Your boat should be secured, at a minimum, by a rope tied across the boat to each side of the rack and by a bow line and a stern line to the front and back bumpers of your car. That way you'll be assured your boat will still be there when you reach the water's edge.

TIP   Hide the keys on or near your car, rather than risk losing them in the water.

Dressing for Success

Regardless of the clothing you wear, you'll get wet, be it from a paddle splash or a complete flip. The possibility of capsizing exists in all waters and it happens when you least expect it. What's more important is staying warm after the splash or soak. Coldness can lead to hypothermia, which is life threatening.

Loose, quick-drying attire is the best clothing for kayaking. Jackets should feel comfortably loose. They shouldn't restrict torso movement while sitting. Choose roomy shorts or pants that don't bind when you sit. Synthetic materials dry quickly and will keep you warmer and more comfortable than wool. Cotton can be used only in the hot summer months because once it's wet, it remains that way, and it loses its insulating ability. Even cotton underwear should be avoided. Most boaters wear a nylon swimsuit under their layers, even in cooler weather.

Be prepared for cooler temperatures and heat loss due to wind. You need to remember that water temperature, rather than air temperature, is the most important consideration. The typical temperature of spring runoff rivers, lakes, and bays can be a frigid 40 °F (4 °C), enough to rob you of your strength after a few minutes of immersion. It's wise to always be prepared for an unexpected swim. As you progress in the sport, you'll need to accumulate enough kayaking apparel to protect you in a wide range of elements. The following items of clothing are advisable, especially for cool weather or cold-water paddling.

Paddling Jacket ($60–$100)

A paddling jacket is made of coated nylon with neck and wrist cuffs to prevent water from dripping into the sleeves and upper body. Made of a windproof fabric, it retains your body heat. Paddling jackets generally are

Dress for an unexpected swim.

not waterproof, yet they can maintain a fair amount of insulating ability if you've been soaked.

Dry Top ($130–$200)

Dry tops are an alternative to paddling jackets. While the tight seals at wrist and neck are less comfortable, the treated synthetic material prevents all water from getting in. Most dry tops feature sealed neoprene closures at the wrists, a tight drawstring at the waist, and a very tight neck seal. While a dry top affords you the luxury of staying warm and dry, it doesn't offer much in comfort. Until it's broken in, the neck seal binds and constricts. After enough wearings the jacket feels comfortable, but the neck seal begins breaking down. Dry tops are generally more expensive than paddling jackets.

Dry Suit ($200–$350)

Dry suits resemble dry tops but have no seal at the waist. Instead they extend down the legs to ankle seals. Dry suits are great; if you end up swimming a lot, they can keep you dry. One disadvantage, as with dry tops, is the discomfort of a tight neck gasket. Also, getting in and out of some of these suits is no easy chore.

Pullover or Sweater ($50–$150)

A synthetic sweater or pullover provides extra insulation and sheds water when wet. Wool provides warmth but stays wet even though it wicks water away from the body. Some pullovers with low cut necks and shorter sleeves are made specifically to wear under paddling jackets.

Farmer John Wet Suit ($50–$150)

The Farmer John wet suit is the paddler's favorite for cold weather wear. Made of neoprene, it is a one piece body suit with thigh- or calf-length legs and a sleeveless top. A zippered front or a Velcro or snap closure at the shoulder allows easy donning and removal. The most popular thickness is 3/16 to 1/4 inch (5–6 mm). The Farmer John is designed to get wet and provides some padding for those unfortunate swims in rocky waters. Its neoprene insulation works best when wet. By keeping a thin layer of water next to your skin, which heats it to your body temperature, your warmth is maintained. For beginning paddlers, the Farmer John wet suit is the best way to go in terms of warmth and durability. Perhaps the best combination is the Farmer John wetsuit with a wool or synthetic sweater covered by a paddling jacket or a dry top.

Footwear ($20–$80)

Protecting your feet from litter on the shore or rocks on the river bottom is very important. Not only will a sturdy-soled shoe or sandal prevent a foot injury, it will enable you to run swiftly after a loose boat slipping downriver or a PFD suddenly caught in the wind. For those starting out in the summer season, an old pair of tennis shoes will do the trick. Ultimately you'll want sturdy plastic or rubber sandals or neoprene booties that are specifically designed for paddling. They keep the sand out and securely protect your feet better than most sandals or tennis shoes.

Headgear ($10–$25)

Almost 75 percent of your body heat escapes through your head and neck. A wool or fleece hat is essential to stay warm on cold days, whether you get wet or stay dry. On the coldest days, a neoprene cap can save your life, especially in the event of a flip. A cheap but very workable alternative is a swimming cap combined with a wool hat.

Handy Accessories

Personal preparedness goes beyond clothing; it includes the accessories that add to your general comfort. A baseball cap or a hat with a wide brim helps protect against the sun. Because water reflects the sun's rays, almost doubling their effects, it's not surprising to hear the unprepared paddler complain of a headache.

However, the sun isn't always the cause of headaches. Sometimes it's water—not drinking enough of it. Since kayakers engage in vigorous activity, their water needs are high though often unnoticed. A water bottle that can tie or clip onto the boat within easy reach is a good hedge against a symptom of dehydration, a headache.

Good quality sunglasses help minimize the glare reflected off the water. Croakies, Chums, or other tie-on straps for your glasses will help keep them on your face. Paddlers who wear contact lenses rather than glasses are at an advantage because they are free to take their sunglasses on and off without interfering with their vision. I use disposable contact lenses and find that they work very well, even in whitewater.

A dry bag or a dry box serves as a waterproof container to protect your extra clothing and food. Available in a wide range of sizes, they can cost anywhere from $10 to $120. A small waterproof bag is useful for storing your sunscreen (an essential), lip balm (preferably the kind with sunscreen), and, depending on its size, a first aid kit. A high energy bar stashed in the bag can give you a needed lift at the end of a long day of paddling.

First Aid Supplies

While carrying your boat to shore, you puncture your foot on a stick poking out of the sand. Scrambling to shore after a flip, you scrape your calf on a rough rock. You cut your thumb while slicing cheese during a lunch stop. Injuries like these—and they are not uncommon—can jeopardize your day of paddling. Don't let the lack of a first aid kit ruin your trip. First aid kits can be purchased for $25 to $100, or you can develop your own kit based on your first aid skills and the remoteness of the paddling you will be doing.

Tailor the amount of first aid gear to the size and needs of your group. Know the medical history of every group member and check on everyone's current health before you leave on a tour, whether it's a day trip or a week-long adventure. Find out if anyone in the group has a known allergy to bee stings, and if so, include an antihistamine kit. A quick exit off a lake or river to seek medical attention can be difficult and sometimes impossible.

 SAFETY TIP If you are thirsty, then your body is a quart (about 1 liter) or more low on fluids. Drink before you get thirsty to stay properly hydrated.

A GEAR LIST

Kayakers have a lot of gear to remember. As an instructor, I've seen many a day ruined when a beginning paddler forgot something. Even simple things like a hat or visor, sunglasses, or water bottle are essential, and showing up with them at the start of your trip helps ensure you'll have a good day.

A Kayaking Gear List
PFD

Paddle

Spray skirt

Boat flotation (air bags or equivalent)

Adequate weather protection for the season:

  Wet suit

  Paddling jacket or dry top

  Booties, poagies (special gloves for hands and paddle), headgear

Sunglasses with strap

Sunscreen

Money

Drinking water

Lunch, extra food

Trip plan filed?

First aid kit

Extra Gear for Sea Kayaking

Spare paddle

Rudder in good working condition?

Tow line

Compass

Navigation charts

Tide tables and tidal current charts

Flares

Air horn or whistle

Waterproof flashlight

Paddle float, rigging, and stirrup

Hand pump and sponge

Extra Gear for Whitewater Kayaking

Throw rope

Rescue knife

Helmet

3

KAYAKING BASICS

Now that you are properly equipped, you are ready to master the basic skills of kayaking. First, you'll learn how to get the boat to the water and enter it in a balanced manner. Then it's time to practice the basic strokes and maneuvers that allow you to control the boat's movement. This chapter provides you with tips to help you paddle efficiently and develop your paddle sensitivity. For simplicity, I believe in learning a minimum number of strokes. Advanced paddlers can talk for hours about subtle ways to place a certain stroke, but four or five basic strokes can perform the majority of all maneuvers needed to get where you want to go.

I'll teach both whitewater and sea kayaking paddling skills in this chapter. Some of these skills are shared between the two styles, but some are unique to the style of paddling you've chosen. Everyone should read this chapter, but then you should focus on your preference of either the whitewater or the sea kayaking techniques and safety.

This chapter will also help you decide how much you're capable of doing your first time out. It'll give you some exercises to increase your flexibility so you'll improve your technique.

Getting Ready

Whether you'll do most of your kayaking on whitewater or on flatwater, you need to learn a few skills before taking that first kayak outing. Practice the skills in this section on some calm water until you've mastered them. Then you'll be well prepared for your next lessons.

Carrying the Boat

You'll see the most experienced paddlers carrying their boat on their shoulders to get down to the water. But there's no reason you shouldn't start by pairing off with someone to carry the boat in tandem. The grab loops at the boat's bow and stern work well as handles for carrying the boat. Avoid straining your lower back by lifting with your legs rather than your back. If you're carrying by yourself, take time to figure out how to use your legs to

Carrying your boat with a partner protects you from back injuries.

bounce the boat up onto your shoulder and to use your foot to snag the paddle and bring it up into your other hand. Sea kayaks are very awkward to carry solo, so nearly everyone pairs up or uses specially designed carts.

Getting Into the Boat

Getting into the kayak on the water without flipping over can be tricky. A sandy beach is an ideal place to put in for the first time. Simply step into the kayak, which should be pointed toward the water, and scoot your way into the water. A rocky shoreline and an expensive boat will force you to put the boat in the water parallel to the shore and use the paddle for stability while getting in. Lay the paddle flat behind your cockpit with one blade up on shore. Stand in front of the paddle shaft with your back to it and reach directly behind you to grab it. Put most of your weight on the part of the paddle that's on the boat, but keep a little bit of weight on the part of the paddle closer to the shore. Step into the boat. Then, slide both legs in at the same time until your bottom rests on the seat.

Putting On the Spray Skirt

Getting the spray skirt, especially a new one, onto the cockpit rim can also be tricky. With your skirt already around your waist, begin from a sitting position and lean back to pull the skirt to your waist or slightly above it. Then reach behind and hook the back of the spray skirt to the rim. Drag your elbows forward and along the skirt, positioning the sides. Reach forward to hook the front of the skirt to the cockpit rim. Make sure to keep the release loop out and accessible. Adjust the sides last. Putting on a skirt can be frustrating, but don't be afraid to ask for help. I've seen people at the starting line of world championships ask for help putting on their spray skirts. It's simply an awkward maneuver that sometimes requires a little assistance.

The Wet Exit

Early in your first day of kayaking, you should learn and practice a wet exit. This is simply swimming out of the boat after it flips over. You should be underwater for only about 5 to 10 seconds. Being relaxed in a kayak demands that you be comfortable hanging out underwater. Practice the wet exit until you can do it in a slow, controlled manner.

Doing a Wet Exit

1. Take a deep breath, flip over, and let go of the paddle.

2. Tuck forward for protection and to orient yourself.

3. Tap your hands on the bottom of the boat three times to relax and remain oriented.

4. Grab the spray skirt release, pull it away from you and off the cockpit.

5. Put your hands on either side of the cockpit rim adjacent to your hips.

6. Push out of the boat like taking off a pair of pants.

7. Push back even more until your legs are free of the cockpit and your PFD can pop you to the surface.

Remain tucked forward when doing a wet exit. A common mistake is leaning back and trying to swim to the surface. This actually tangles your legs and makes the wet exit feel more difficult and rushed than necessary.

After your first few wet exits, get a friend to help you empty the water out of your boat. Then, after a little practice, you can try placing one end of the boat on shore and lifting the other end to drain water by yourself. Lift with your legs to avoid back injury!

Balancing Skills

Before working on specific strokes and moves, start by making sure your position in the boat is relaxed and balanced. Remember to use good posture to allow a full torso twist. Sit comfortably with your chest forward and chin up.

Balance is obviously an important part of kayaking. If your whole body is stiff, you'll flip over. To balance easily and use a wide variety of strokes, you'll need to be flexible. Gently stretch your muscles before and after you paddle. (See the following section on "Getting Fit for Kayaking" for some suggested stretches for improving flexibility for paddling.) Practicing leans and putting the boat on edge will help you develop good balance.

Leans, and the resulting good balance, are an important part of learning to paddle, but they are rarely described with precision. Leans can be categorized into three types: the bell buoy lean, the body lean, and the J lean.

The bell buoy lean is named for the stiff rocking action of an ocean bell buoy. Navigation bell buoys are so bottom heavy that they are self-righting.

Kayaks aren't that way, so keeping a stiff torso makes your boat wobble like a bell buoy. Either you will flip, or momentarily catch yourself with the paddle and then flip. This makes it an inappropriate lean.

The body lean leaves the boat level while the body leans. Beginners like this lean since the boat feels secure. Unfortunately, a level boat usually defeats the purpose of the lean. Beginning paddlers are easily fooled into thinking they are tilting the boat when in fact they are just leaning their body. Body leans rarely serve any useful purpose.

The best lean to use is the J lean. In a J lean, named for the shape of your spine when the lean is done correctly, your weight is centered over the boat. This lean keeps most of the weight off your blade so you can use it for balance and for strokes.

The three types of leans are the J lean (left), the body lean (center), and the bell buoy lean (right).

Learning and practicing the J lean is best done on flatwater. First, lean in your boat and feel how the weight and pressure change from both knees to just one. Thrust out your ribs and physically torque up the opposite knee. Feel how the weight and pressure change from both sides of your bottom to just one. Keep your body comfortably relaxed over the boat with your head centered over its middle. Notice how a good J lean requires that your head be cocked away from the direction of the lean. Tilting the boat with a J lean is known as *putting the boat on edge*, or *edging*.

Now rock the boat over to edge on the other side and try the same maneuver. This will give you a good feel for the boat's stability. Master kayakers don't rely on their paddle for support, even with their boats on edge.

If these drills are difficult, you might practice the C stretches for the torso discussed later in the chapter.

Taking Your First Stroke

Holding the paddle correctly will increase your stroke power and decrease your chance of overuse injury. The offset blades (see p. 23) determine how you grip the paddle shaft. Many sea kayakers adjust the offset of their paddles to alleviate arm strain. Paddling with unfeathered paddles is also common in sea kayaking. But we will assume that you are using the more common offset paddle.

One hand is the control hand and remains indexed, that is, it stays in the same place on the shaft. Ninety-five percent of paddles (except in Eastern Europe) are right-hand controlled. Some people prefer left-hand controlled paddles. However, there's little evidence that a left-control paddle will ease your learning, regardless of which hand is dominant for you. In the stroke descriptions that follow, we assume you will be using a right-control paddle. Simply reverse the directions if you're using a left-control paddle.

Every stroke includes both a push with one arm and a pull with the other. Your control hand holds the shaft with the top of your knuckles lined up with the upper edge of the blade. This orientation ensures that during a right-side stroke, your right forearm continues pulling in the desired direction. The opposite hand has a relaxed grip so the paddle can rotate in that hand. Your left arm pushes the stroke through. Left-side strokes begin by cocking your control hand wrist down (like revving a motorcycle). This movement turns the left blade to the position for a forward stroke. During the pull of this stroke you'll be gripping and pulling with your left hand while your right hand pushes. For a right-side stroke, relax the left hand and rotate the paddle shaft back into position with the right hand. Keeping the fingers extended on the top arm, the pushing arm, allows a fluid movement.

TECHNIQUE TIP   A common paddling error is holding the shaft with a two-handed death grip. This is tiring and ineffective. Remember to relax the noncontrol hand during every stroke. Let the paddle shaft rotate freely between strokes.

Stroke Techniques

Knowing how to edge the boat, sit up straight, and hold the paddle correctly are all prerequisites to developing a kayaking finesse. Once you have mastered them, you can begin to focus on stroke technique. The best boaters are fanatics about their strokes, practicing and fine-tuning them on flat, easy water.

LEARNING TIP — With any stroke, think of your torso as the engine, your arms as the transmission, and your paddle blade as the wheels of a car. Too often paddlers use their arms as the engine and don't have a smooth transmission of power. The result is tired arms and ineffective strokes.

All strokes should be done with your arms stationed comfortably in front of your body. This position prevents your arms from becoming overextended or awkwardly placed. During strokes that sweep to the boat's end, you will turn your torso to keep your arms in the proper position.

I'll start your stroke lesson by describing sweep strokes, which turn the boat and help you control your direction. Then we will study the forward

Proper technique for holding a right-control paddle.

stroke and some tricks for keeping the boat going straight. Draw strokes to move sideways and reverse paddling will round out our stroke lesson.

Forward Sweep

A well-developed forward sweep stroke enables you to reach your paddling potential. Used to turn the boat, forward sweep strokes incorporate three principles: They are powered by the large muscle groups of the torso, they follow a full 180-degree arc, and they require a solid purchase on the water.

Reach with torso rotation before you plant the blade (top left). Extend in an arc 3 ft (1 m) from the boat (top right). Watch the blade to the stern to extend the stroke's effectiveness (bottom).

The strong muscles that connect your torso to the lower body power this stroke, while arm muscles are reserved for small, subtle adjustments. Torso rotation enables you to harness this large muscle group. Twist your torso and extend the blade forward. Straighten the arm near the water and pull your other hand back and below your shoulder. Plant the blade completely in the water, then unwind your torso. As you reach the end of a comfortable twist, lift the edge of the boat on the side of your stroke. Lift your knee as you drive your forward hand across the deck of the boat.

During the sweep, the blade should travel in an arc extending about 3 feet (0.9 m) from the boat. In order to do this, both hands should start below shoulder level. Make sure the top of the blade remains submerged throughout the stroke. To maintain your torso rotation, watch your blade as it sweeps all the way to the back. Pay close attention to ensure the blade stays straight up, not at an angle, in the water. Without an adjustment by cocking your wrist, the blade has a tendency to twist at the end of the stroke, reducing its bite on the water.

Transfer the power into your boat with your legs by pushing on the sweeping side's foot brace and pulling your hip towards the blade. Practice forward sweep strokes while the boat is flat and while it's on edge.

Many sea kayaks have rudders that can help with a gradual turn. Push on the left pedal to turn left. For a tight turn in a sea kayak you will not use the rudder. Instead, tilt the boat way up on edge, away from the direction of the turn.

How you apply power is important as well. Yanking the paddle simply pulls it through the water. A solid hold on the water by the paddle blade allows the boat to move effectively. Bubbles or splashes behind the blade are an indication that you're pulling too fast. Notice how well your boat turns when the blade grabs the water securely.

Stern Draw

The last part of the sweep stroke is so important and so frequently botched that instructors often isolate it by calling it a stern draw. For the purposes of practice, it's important to move your sweep stroke in a full 180-degree arc from bow to stern. But often you will vary the length of the sweep to control how much the boat turns. For instance, the back portion of the sweep is used to pull the stern around without moving the boat forward. This is the stern draw.

A common mistake is to hold the paddle at an angle that simply lifts water and doesn't move the stern around. I recommend that you punch across your body with your top hand, twist your torso with the stroke, and watch the blade as you pull it all the way in toward the boat.

Reverse Sweep

Occasionally, for a quick turn you will use a reverse sweep. This is simply the opposite of the forward version. Use the opposite side of the blade, and provide most of the power while your torso unwinds from back to front. Linking the forward and reverse sweep strokes, one on each side, can provide a crisp turn. Practice this turn and critique how smoothly you are doing the motion. This stroke combination is great for turning around. The first few inches of a reverse sweep can act as a rudder. This rudder stroke is particularly useful when surfing on a river, or in the ocean.

In a short whitewater boat you will be able to spin easily and fast enough to get dizzy. In a sea kayak the turn will be slow, like jockeying your car around in a narrow driveway.

Going Forward

When you first tried paddling forward, you probably used your small, nimble arm muscles to provide all your power. A better strategy is to incorporate larger muscles for a more powerful, efficient stroke. Sound familiar? As in sweep strokes, forward strokes depend on power that originates from torso rotation. The challenge is keeping the blade perpendicular to the side of the boat, which results in an efficient pull forward. This blade position minimizes the turning effect. The further away the blade is positioned, like in a sweep stroke, the more the boat will turn.

To begin the stroke, lead with your chest; the bigger the twist, the better. Get extra blade extension by bending your top arm. Concentrate on getting the blade crisply and fully submerged in the water before pulling yourself forward. Use the power of your leg and torso muscles before allowing your bottom arm to bend. Push on the foot brace for extra power. Strive to achieve a smooth, gliding sensation without any front-to-back bobbing. Pull the blade out as it reaches your hip, and wind up for the stroke on the other side.

LEARNING TIP

Torso rotation is easily learned while sitting in front of a mirror. This allows you to monitor how much you are rotating and to feel the rhythm of movement without having to deal with keeping your boat stable or straight.

Imagine sitting in your boat and reaching forward to start a lawn mower. This twisting front-to-back reach is the source of the torso and hip power needed for kayaking. However, using that power is tricky. Too much front-to-back motion bobs the boat and jeopardizes your control and efficiency. Instead, use torso rotation, twisting around your spine to provide the pull of each stroke.

A quality forward stroke uses torso rotation in a smooth, symmetrical motion.

Let's look a little more closely at the hand positions for a forward stroke. Equally skilled paddlers enjoy endless debates on the merits of a power stroke with a high top hand and a touring stroke with both hands kept low.

For short boats, short distances, and high speeds, people tend to use a shorter paddle that allows a higher shaft angle; the top hand remains high, between shoulder and eye level. For shorter sprints, like paddling in whitewater or ocean surf, you need this powerful forward stroke.

For extended paddling, the forward stroke is more relaxed; the top hand drops, the elbows drop, and the stroke comes back a little further instead of being extended toward the front. In the touring forward stroke, propelling the boat becomes secondary to reducing the effort you have to expend. To paddle large distances, you will find lots of stroke variations and explore different ways to keep the boat moving.

Going Straight

Paddling in a straight line may be your first frustration in kayaking. The boat may seem to have a mind of its own, twisting into tighter and tighter turns with each stroke. Although a sea kayak may have a rudder to help the paddler follow a straight path, well-executed strokes are useful to maintain the line.

When the boat starts to turn, a solid sweep or stern draw on the side you're turning to corrects this. Be sure to line up on a distant landmark so you realize early that the boat is turning. With experience, you will anticipate a turn and correct it before the boat starts to spin. Don't waste energy trying to correct by making stronger forward strokes.

TO GO FASTER: PADDLE IN MOLASSES

Speed from a standstill is the key to kayaking in all waters. Think of your boat as gliding in a giant vat of molasses. Each stroke will stick securely in the water to move you quickly and efficiently. By imagining the blade pulling against molasses, you will develop the stroke needed to effectively pull the boat forward.

The blade in molasses analogy can provide the answers to commonly asked questions about the length and speed of forward strokes. The blade should be planted as far forward as your torso twist allows in order to pull yourself forward the greatest distance. Don't pull until the blade is fully immersed. When the blade reaches your hip, the power phase of the stroke is completed and the recovery begins. Simply increasing your stroke rate won't necessarily make your boat go faster. To go faster, concentrate on pulling carefully while the blade is in the water, then recover quickly for the next blade plant.

To practice these concepts with your forward stroke, try flatwater paddling alongside a series of fixed markers like dock pilings or buoys. The blade should enter the water cleanly with minimal splash. Watch how much the blade slips with each stroke. It should hardly move at all while you move past. You should consistently feel resistance against the blade. Remember the blade in molasses analogy!

Draw Stroke

Occasionally, you'll want to move sideways. A basic stroke for this is the draw stroke. Turn your torso and place the blade straight out from your hip. With both hands over the water, push out with the top hand as you pull the blade in toward the boat. Tilt your boat away slightly. Rotate the blade 90 degrees for the recovery.

A sculling draw accomplishes the same movement and is a good exercise to help you feel the effects of subtle changes in blade angle. Rotate the blade as you move it back-and-forth along a 2-foot (61-cm) line 6 inches (15 cm) away from and parallel to your boat, making sure to keep the shaft straight up and down. Gradually open the blade angle on the forward portion of the stroke, then rotate it so the leading edge is open as you bring the blade back. Don't try to pull in on the blade or apply too much force. Your goal is a maximum sideways pull on the boat with a minimum resistance to moving the blade.

A draw stroke pulls your boat sideways.

Reverse Paddling

Important for stopping and maneuvering, reverse paddling complements your other strokes. Without changing your grip, use the opposite side of the blade and the same techniques as for forward paddling.

Rolling

The Inuit developed the roll as a lifesaving move in freezing waters, hence the term "Eskimo roll." At times, an entire Inuit family and all their belongings would be stowed under the deck. A roll could save the whole family. Modern-day recreational paddlers use the same move as a convenient self-rescue on friendlier waters. During remote touring trips or on difficult water, the roll can still be a lifesaver.

Knowing how to roll will help you avoid inconvenient and unnecessary wet exits. Whether you are a long way from shore or are being swept downstream on a river, the presence of mind required for a roll is worth it. You don't stay immersed as long, so you stay warmer and can quickly continue on your way.

No maneuver in kayaking intrigues beginning paddlers as much as the roll. For most, the challenge of learning the move intensifies its mystique. Some paddlers learn to roll in one lesson, others take weeks.

There are actually two subtly different variations of rolling. In one style of rolling, the C-to-C, you position your body and paddle perpendicular to the overturned boat before any righting action begins. In the other style of rolling, the sweep, the righting action occurs while the paddle sweeps to perpendicular. Paddlers can be quite passionate about their own way of rolling, so don't let different explanations confuse you. For simplicity, I'll only describe the C-to-C roll.

To help you learn the progression of the roll, I've broken the instruction down into two parts. In the first part, you'll learn how to do the hip snap without the paddle while your body remains out of the water. Then we'll work on the roll as you're underwater holding a paddle.

Hip Snap

The objective of every good roll is to move the boat right-side up first, so your body can follow. The key is doing this with little support from the paddle. Minimizing paddle involvement in the roll depends on a solid hip snap, in which the torso and knee motion rights the boat.

The best way to practice the hip snap is in the boat along the side of a pool or a low dock. Have a partner help you with this exercise. A qualified instructor is the best assistant.

To wind up for a hip snap, relax your torso so the boat flops over on you, almost upside down. Then follow through by gently pressing your right ear toward your shoulder and tugging up on your right knee. Your left knee relaxes, barely even touching the deck. You should have almost no pressure on the left foot pedal. If you are hanging onto the boat with both knees, you defeat the hip action and the entire motion will feel strained. Think of the pressure changing from one side of your bottom to the other. Practice rotating the boat through a full 180-degree range of motion.

This motion should feel very natural before you try rolling with a paddle. Note how little effort it takes to right the boat when you keep your weight floating near the surface and rotate the boat up with your hips, knees, and torso. Think light! Be sure not to push your body up with your arms or lift your head.

To become better acquainted with the body's position in a roll, turn your boat over while your partner stands behind your cockpit holding your torso out to the right while your head remains just above the water's surface. Practice your hip snap from this position.

A hip snap is the key to righting the boat in practice and in rolls. For a quality hip snap, right the boat with your knee and torso, not your arms!

C-to-C Roll

When you've mastered the hip snap, you're ready to practice the roll. The essence of the C-to-C roll is the same as the hip snap. The curvature of the torso from one side of the kayak to the other rights an upside-down kayak.

To start a roll, first capsize the boat and get in the protected forward tucked position, called the set-up. Tuck tight. Place your paddle with the blade power face up and the shaft parallel to the left seam line. Your wrists will be on the left side of the boat.

Your torso has to lead the arm motion. Any roll you do will rely on positioning the paddle with your torso more than your arms. Open up your body and arch your back to roll your torso out to your left side. This gets you really wound up into position for a hip snap. Then relax the knee that pulled you into the wind-up and rotate the boat up with your hip snap.

An assistant can help you position the paddle when you're learning the roll (top). Your torso and knee motion right the boat.

LEARNING TIP   Concentrate on minimizing the force on the blade. Somehow this is a hard concept for us to remember underwater. Instead of pulling the paddle down, think of following the blade with your upper body.

Once you have learned the roll, practice it hundreds of times on flatwater. Decide deliberately to stay in your boat unless you know of a specific hazard. Don't rush. Wait until you can feel cool air on your hands in the set-up position. Go methodically through the rolling motion. On flatwater you can practice reacting to the rushed sensation of an accidental flip by purposely flipping at high speed or with only one hand on the shaft. Don't use your roll to get in over your head, so to speak, in terms of your skill. Being in control is much more fun than counting fish! Whitewater paddlers, remember to wear your helmet.

Bow Rescues

The hip snap motion is also the foundation for bow rescues, where the rescue boat quickly maneuvers to a position perpendicular to the flipped boat. The upside-down paddler scans for the bow of the rescuing boat and reaches up on both sides to grasp it. Once both hands have a firm grasp of the bow, the position is similar to the hip snap practiced by the side of the pool. Right the boat with a strong hip snap without lifting your head or pushing up with your arms.

This is a fairly common rescue method used in hazard-free whitewater, where an attentive friend or instructor can help you stay in your boat. In sea kayaking, bow rescues are used only as practice, since a sea kayak's limited maneuverability prevents impromptu moving into position.

Bracing

The brace is a defensive maneuver that can keep you right-side up. The blade rests (or slaps) on the water to allow a hip snap to right the boat. A brace requires a fair amount of paddle dexterity and timing, so don't be surprised if you actually learn to roll first.

A common misconception is that leverage, getting your head up, and pressure on the blade are the keys to a good brace. This is all wrong! Easy braces require that you keep the shaft horizontal and slide the blade in close to the boat to make it easy to slide your weight over the boat. Move the blade inboard, closer to the boat, to help center your weight over the boat.

Low Brace

When you watch someone making a successful low brace it may appear that the paddle brings the boat right-side up. This isn't quite right. The paddle offers only momentary support while your torso and knee motion rights the boat. For a low brace you will use the back, or nonpower, face of the blade. Your elbows will be directly above your hands.

Using a low brace to sidesurf.

High Brace

A good high brace commits your body to the water, with your elbows low and a minimum of force on your shoulders and blade. Your hands are directly above your elbows. Throw your head to the water to exaggerate the hip snap motion, and curve toward that side. Then, to recover, you can slink your body and head up over the upright boat.

Hanging on with a high brace in a big hole.

For safe and effective rolls and braces, your hands shouldn't move more than a couple inches from your shoulders. Your elbows should act like shock absorbers, so keep the shaft in front of your shoulders. Use smooth finesse rather than power. Overextension of your arms in an attempt to get more leverage makes rolls and braces harder, because it pulls your head and torso off center. Plus it exposes your arm and shoulder to injury. The safe finishing position for braces and rolls is with your elbows low and in close to your body. Don't worry if you don't save yourself with a brace or a roll. Equally important are good self-rescue skills.

SAFETY TIP   If you have shoulder problems, seek experienced instruction to help you learn the brace. If you don't have shoulder problems, seek experienced instruction to help you avoid shoulder problems!

Keep Your Head Down!

Lifting your head to breathe is the most common ailment of bow rescues, braces, and rolls. You must believe! If the head comes up, the boat stays down. Don't rush to get air. It won't help. Instead, use your head to make effective moves; let it be the last thing to clear the water. This counterintuitive motion involves flexibility and rarely used muscles. Allow plenty of time to practice it—some people learn it in one day, but others work on it throughout a season.

Learn at Your Own Pace

As an instructor, I find it disturbing to see paddlers who are pushed into aspects of the sport that are beyond their abilities. A classic example of this is people getting taken on more and more difficult rivers with their friends, even though those rivers are beyond their skill level. It's important to use a good learning progression, first paddling easy trips then moving on to more difficult ones as you progress.

The following checklist will help ensure that you learn the sport at a good pace. If you're not accustomed to learning new sports, you might want to plan your first kayaking experience to be an easy day, maybe just an hour or two. On the other hand, if you're an athletic person, quick to learn different sports, you can have a good full day of it your first time out.

LEARNING CHECKLIST FOR BEGINNING PADDLERS

- Take a lesson. Even a 2-day lesson can give you a solid understanding of safety and save you from some unpleasant experiences.

- Be thirsty for information. Ask lots of questions, read books, watch training videos.

- Try before you buy! Trying equipment and talking to others in your area will help you focus your paddling interests.

- Pick your paddling partners carefully. Experts aren't always the best teachers, and rarely is a spouse, boyfriend, or girlfriend the best choice.

- Be realistic in appraising your skill and experience level.

Getting Fit for Kayaking

Kayaking can be done at nearly any level of intensity. For a short paddle, you can jump in a boat for a quick hour of exercise on a nearby lake, flatwater river, or quiet ocean bay. This can be a relaxing cruise or a wind sprint designed to improve your strength and cardiovascular fitness.

A Fitness Program

The best fitness program for kayaking is paddling. "As much as possible, time in the boat" is the motto borrowed from European elite-level paddlers. This is because of the cardinal rule of sports training: Specificity. The more specific your preparations, the better your performance.

In addition to using kayaking to improve your fitness, you can also condition your body beforehand to enhance your experience. Improved physical fitness will make your paddling more enjoyable because you'll feel more energetic and be able to paddle greater distances without fatigue. You'll feel stronger and be better able to do routine tasks like carrying boats and dealing with unexpected difficulties like increasing winds. You'll also feel more flexible and be able to use your entire body to execute your strokes strongly and efficiently.

For all these reasons, your paddling will benefit from a general fitness program at the local sports or fitness club. Aerobics and strength training will give you more general endurance when you're in the boat. Ask one of the club's fitness consultants to teach you a routine for general fitness. With their help you might add a few upper-body exercises specifically to aid your paddling.

Stretches

I like to use stretches that relate specifically to the movements I'll do in the boat. Whether you train on the water or in a local sports club, the following three stretches are recommended as very beneficial for your comfort and kayaking efficiency. These stretch your torso in the three directions you can move in a kayak. Before you do these stretches, warm up for a few minutes with some light running or paddling motions. Then stretch gently, just to the point where you feel the stretch. Hold this position for 15 to 20 seconds. Repeat three times in each direction. Stretching before each paddle helps prevent injuries like tendinitis, muscle soreness, strains, and dislocations. Stretching afterwards can improve your flexibility.

C STRETCHES   Stand with your feet slightly apart. Raise your hands above your head and interlace your fingers. Slowly lower your arms to the side so that your body makes the shape of a *C*. You should feel the stretch in the side you're leaning away from.

TORSO TWISTS   Sit in the boat or on the ground with your legs in front of you and your back straight. Twist your chest and shoulders and concentrate on feeling the stretch low and deep in your torso. If you do the stretch in the boat, you can grasp the deck: one hand in front of you, one behind.

HAMSTRING STRETCHES   Lie flat on your back with your knees bent. Lift and straighten one leg and grab it near the ankle, gently pulling it toward you. If you have trouble reaching your leg with your hands, use a towel or a short section of webbing.

SAFETY TIP   Warm up and stretch before each paddle. Be systematic about gradually increasing the distance and difficulty you tackle. Remember to cool down and stretch after each paddle.

4

WHITEWATER KAYAKING TECHNIQUES AND SAFETY

Whatever your whitewater kayaking destination—maneuvering through a steep gorge, crashing through large standing waves, or merely playing on small surf waves—you'll need a set of techniques to help keep you safe and to keep the trip pleasurable. If you are a dedicated sea kayaker unlikely to try any whitewater, you may skip this chapter and proceed to the sea kayaking techniques in chapter 5.

Reading Water

At first glance it looks like the thrill of whitewater is the pure exhilaration of crashing down through waves and big drops. But that is only part of the excitement. Reading the river, figuring out how your boat will react, then picking your line become a rewarding challenge. This skill takes considerable experience, but in most ideal learning situations all that happens from misreading is you flip over or simply bounce over a rock. Learning to read a river's features will help you determine its friendliness.

I remember my first day behind the wheel in driver's education class. Heading out of the school driveway, I had my eyes riveted to the hood of the car. As the car ran up on the curb, the instructor grabbed the wheel, screaming for me to look down the road. A lengthy lecture on scanning the road followed my mistake. Learning to paddle whitewater can be a similar experience. Reading the road and reading the river actually have a lot in common.

The key to reading water is to lift your line of vision! Don't just look at your bow. Look where you want to go and at what lies in between. What should you be looking for? Simple: easily visible rocks, water features formed by rocks under the surface, and hazards.

As you scan the rapid, look far downstream to figure out where the current ends. Does the main flow enter on one side but finish in a wave bouncing on the other side? You might see some rocks above the water deflecting the current, for example. Figuring out why the current was deflected is the key to reading the rapid.

An instructor can help you learn to identify natural river hazards like undercut rocks or artificial things like bridge pilings. Tree branches forming strainers are one of the most dangerous hazards in the sport. Scan for bouncing twigs and unexplained currents that might indicate a strainer. Learn to identify potential danger spots, then concentrate on where you want to go rather than on what you want to avoid.

Learning to read water takes time and practice, so paddle within your ability and experience. Don't just follow other boaters. Instead, explore easy, safe rapids by picking your own line.

Visible Rocks

Beginner paddlers are usually terrified of the rocks in the river. Rocks won't bite. In fact, they rarely pose a significant danger. You can spot them easily and turn to avoid them. You usually won't plan to hit rocks, but if you do hit one, it's important to react properly.

If you find yourself floating sideways toward a rock, lean your body and boat aggressively toward the rock, even putting your hand or paddle on it. The water buffeting off the rock forms a pillow which helps keep your boat off the rock. A round rock tends to be friendlier than one with a sharp upstream edge. Learn to distinguish between them.

Eddies

Just downstream of a rock is a quiet spot, called an eddy. The eddy is a paddler's refuge from the current and is the most important water feature to know and understand. Paddlers use eddies to stop and rest, to scout an upcoming rapid, and for access to fun play spots. The transition area between the current and the eddy is known as the eddy line.

Paddlers use eddies as safe refuge.

Holes

A hole or hydraulic is formed by water flowing over a submerged rock. The resulting water feature is either a hole or a wave, depending on how much water is pouring over.

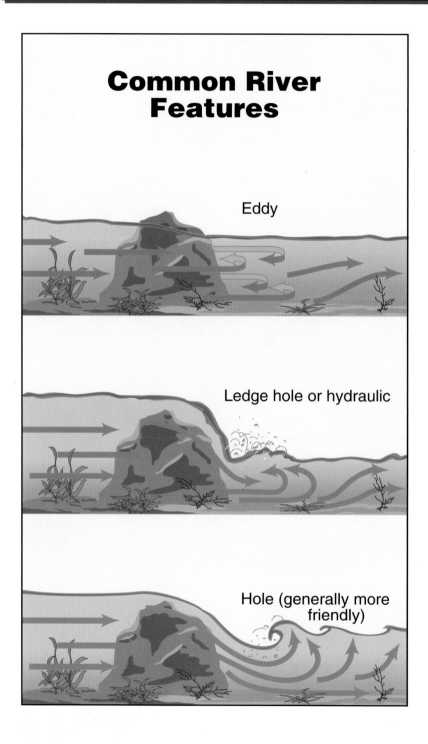

Common River Features

Eddy

Ledge hole or hydraulic

Hole (generally more friendly)

A little water flowing over the rock leaves a very calm, strong eddy below and a very shallow hole, often called a hydraulic. More water flowing over the rock generates a hole, a wavelike formation with a white, frothy backwash. Variations are referred to as stoppers, reversals, keepers, pour-overs, and ledge holes.

To evaluate holes, look downstream and beyond to see clues in the current. Is it wavelike, with water splashing up, implying a sloping entry to a fun play hole? Or is it flat with a horizon line, suggesting that it rushes to a steep drop and pours over into a ledge hole? Watch for water pouring steeply over a rock into a hydraulic and flowing out with the calm look of an eddy. This hole will be less friendly. The amount of water rushing back upstream is a measure of the hole's power.

If you see current splashing downstream, the hole will look more like a wave, indicating deep water. The more a hole resembles a wave, the friendlier it will be. Whitewater dancing up and waves just downstream from the hole are friendly characteristics to watch for. If your path takes you into a hole, plan to hit it straight on, perpendicular to the ledge. Reach your strokes over the backwash and dig into the downstream current. Paddle through it!

Horizon Lines

Occasionally, the water will seem to disappear over the edge of a drop. This horizon line indicates a big drop, one that you will probably want to scout from shore. From a safe place, look for the biggest waves in the main flow of current. Generally, those will direct you to a clear channel and the most fun.

Whitewater Maneuvers

Learn to use rocks, eddies, and holes to run a rapid gracefully, and to play in the rapid. Let's take a quick look at some of the basic whitewater maneuvers.

Ferrying

A ferry is a maneuver that gets you across the river, from an eddy on one side to an eddy on the other side. While this is practical for maneuvering, the ferry is best because it can move you into fun surf waves. You start in an eddy, facing upstream.

To start a ferry, position yourself nearly parallel to the eddy line. This position is often the most important part of the ferry. Achieving this position requires paddle control and finesse. Backing up, then drawing or sculling may be necessary to move into place. With experience, you will learn to jockey into position.

Once you are positioned close to the eddy line, start looking at the current direction and speed. The current next to the eddy line has usually been deflected by rocks, so it flows in a different direction than the main flow. Establish an upstream angle for aiming your boat across the current. That angle depends on the speed of the water: the faster the current, the more you'll need to point straight upstream. If you are unsure of the angle, pointing straight upstream is most conservative. The goal is to cross the current while keeping your bow from getting pushed downstream.

Crossing the eddy line is a crucial point in keeping your ferry angle. The bow is in the current but the stern is in the eddy, so different forces are acting on your boat. Maintaining good forward speed reduces the time these forces have to alter your course.

Stroke timing and placement are important. The instant your feet reach the oncoming current you should be poised for a stern draw correction on the downstream side of your boat, in case your boat turns downstream. Realize the importance of correcting the angle from the stern when ferrying. The stern draw, the end of the forward sweep, works with the current to turn the stern of the boat. The first part of a sweep stroke doesn't correct a ferry angle as well since it pushes the bow against the current.

Another option for correcting the boat angle is a rudder stroke on the upstream side of the kayak. Use good form with the rudder stroke, rotating the blade close to the boat then pushing away slightly. Set the blade on edge, like a sailboat tiller. This requires rolling your wrists back and a slight counterbalance lean away from the stroke. Don't do an inadvertent reverse stroke and put on the brakes when you want the easy turn of a rudder. A sloppy, poorly executed rudder stroke slows the boat and makes it tippy.

Once you have crossed the eddy line with either a rudder or stern draw, you can open up your angle and paddle directly toward the eddy on the other side of the river. Well-executed ferries give you a feeling of control on the river.

Eddy Turns

Eddy turns are the foundation for controlling the speed of your descent down the river. In the quiet of an eddy, you can look at the rest of the rapid, rest, line up for your next move, or get out to portage. By paddling into the eddy at the correct angle with a bit of speed and then tilting the boat up on edge, you'll remain right-side up and feel secure.

The proper line of approach into an eddy gets you there, not a magic set of strokes. This requires setting your approach angle well in advance of the rock and its eddy. Take into account that the current usually bounces off rocks just before the eddy line. This changes the water direction and speed, pushing your bow away from the eddy. By watching the current as it hits the rock and is deflected, you can see the eddy line more easily. Study the size and shape of the rock to anticipate the changing current.

Position the boat slightly sideways to the current and keep your momentum. Sometimes you will need to pause briefly before accelerating into the eddy. It will look as if you are going to hit the rock. Take whatever strokes are necessary to penetrate deep into the eddy. Sometimes a sweep on the downstream side is needed to compensate for the current deflected off the rock. Other times a sweep on the upstream side keeps the boat from turning early. Be sure to allow the bow of the boat to stick into the eddy before initiating a turn.

Upon entering the eddy, tilt the boat in order to stay balanced. Start leaning into the turn when your feet cross the eddy line. Gradually level the boat as you turn upstream.

Your approach path should land you high and deep in the eddy, away from the eddy line. This will require aggressive forward speed. If you finish your turn close to the eddy line, or lower where the eddy is less distinctly formed, you'll risk slipping out the bottom. This will make you feel out of control until you regain speed and find another stopping place.

PRACTICE THE EDDY TURN

1. Set your angle of approach.
2. Build (or keep) momentum toward the eddy.
3. Tilt your boat into the turn as you cross the eddy line.

Peel-outs

Peel-outs are the moves done to leave an eddy and head downstream. Odds are that your first peel-out will be by accident, while trying to cross the eddy in a ferry. Your peel-outs from the eddy should be fun and precise. The departure path from the eddy is almost identical to a ferry but at a slightly wider angle relative to the current and eddy line. Use strokes that position the boat at the proper angle and keep the boat from turning until you've crossed the eddy line.

Peel out of the eddy in the trough of a wave, rather than climbing up the back of a wave. If your boat isn't positioned properly and with enough speed for the exit, it will be turned rapidly on the eddy line. This is a wobbly place to be.

You'll be told to lean downstream while crossing the eddy line. This isn't quite true; your boat should lean, not you. Lift the upstream knee and ride on one cheek of your bottom. In this position you'll be edging the boat just enough to keep from flipping. The faster the current, the greater the tilt needed to remain balanced. When finishing the turn, gradually shift your weight onto both cheeks to level out the boat.

TECHNIQUE TIP   "Lean downstream" is the most common advice given to beginner paddlers. Remember, this only applies to maintaining your stability when leaving an eddy. If you leaned all the time, you'd rarely feel balanced! Think of tilting your boat, rather than leaning your body.

Floating Sideways

On occasion, you will position your boat sideways, at an angle to the rapid you're running. This will allow you to paddle forward to get to one side of the river, and backwards to get to the other. Your downstream momentum will be lessened and the river obstacles won't seem to come at you as quickly. But you need to turn straight to avoid the instability of hitting a rock or ledge hole sideways.

Surfing

To surf, look for a wave that starts right next to an eddy. You'll ferry from the eddy into position on the wave so your boat is actually sliding down the wave. The key to getting on a wave is knowing exactly where to aim when leaving the eddy, and controlling your boat position in the wave trough.

First, leave the eddy in a ferry. Aim for the depression on the eddy line in between the peaks of the waves. This is where the trough of the wave meets the eddy. Position your boat so you are sitting on the wave with your feet in the trough. Feel for the sensation of your bow dropping down into the trough. Monitor the distance between the bow and the ramp of oncoming water. Try to skim the bow of your boat along that dark water.

Surfing a wave—one of the thrills of kayaking.

When surfing some waves, the water will pour over several inches of your deck—don't let the bow dig in by applying too much power. The bow stays dry while surfing other waves. The instant the bow rises up, or slips back, take hard forward strokes to stay on the wave. Keep your boat pointed straight upstream into the oncoming current with stern draw or light rudder strokes. Imagine yourself surfing down the trough of a wave. Notice the sensation and view when you slide off the wave. How do you correct it? What do you do when your bow digs in? What strokes move your bow to the right? . . . to the left?

Sidesurfing

Sidesurfing is a great way to play on the river and to get an understanding about holes. The goal is to sit sideways in a hydraulic, using the wave shape to hold you in position. You will be free to move if your balance comes from posture and knee lift, rather than a heavily weighted paddle, which will make you feel stuck.

Easy sidesurfing holes resemble waves with a shallow entry angle on the upstream side. Even a tall wave can offer a gentle ride if its entry is shallow. Initially, avoid holes such as pour-overs in which the water moves smoothly back upstream. Where the water falls steeply, a smooth ride is unlikely. In addition, a steep entry angle requires a strong boat edge resulting in a weighted paddle. The length of the backwash is a factor in evaluating a sidesurfing hole's strength. The longer, the stronger and more dangerous.

The best sidesurfing is done with the boat edged and your head and body balanced over the boat. Unfortunately, many paddlers instinctively place

Playing in holes tests your skills and can add to the fun on the river.

the paddle far away from the boat for outrigger-type support. The flaw of this approach is that the blade keeps sinking. The more the blade reaches from the boat, the more the head and shoulders move off-center, and the more paddle pressure is needed to stay upright.

Simply find a balance point where pressure on the blade is unnecessary. Use just enough edge to keep the boat from flipping upstream. Stay loose in the hips for the ride. Tight muscles tire quickly, and balance is lost. Don't allow tension inside your boat. Your body should feel relaxed and balanced over the boat. Remember to breathe!

For safety, your arms should be held low, elbows well below the shoulders and in front of your torso. Shoulder dislocations are infrequent, but are the most common injury in kayaking. They happen during extended arm positions. During torso rotation your elbows should remain in front of your shoulders and close to your body. Be especially careful to avoid upstream braces in shallow holes. Instead, tuck your head tight to the cockpit as you flip. If you feel stuck trying to move the paddle around while sidesurfing, you are probably leaning out over the water, stiff, like a bell buoy. Instead, move the blade closer to the boat to center your weight.

For balancing, use only gentle pressure on the paddle. Also try moving forward and backward in the hole. Use the blade in high brace or low brace positions.

Whitewater Safety

One component of whitewater safety is knowing how to swim in fast water. Under an instructor's supervision, practice swimming on your back, with feet at the surface pointing downstream. This safe swimming position helps prevent trapping your feet on the bottom of the river. Your kayak training routine should include learning other aggressive swimming techniques and self-rescue skills. One important skill is learning to swim aggressively with a side stroke to the safest eddy or shoreline.

Also important is learning how to accept help from an experienced kayaker. When appropriate, an experienced kayaker will offer the end of his or her boat to help tow you to shore. Listen carefully to the directions you're given and help by kicking. You should also learn and practice accepting a rope thrown for rescue, as ropes are sometimes stationed at rescue spots in tricky rapids or used to retrieve paddlers stranded in the middle.

Successfully running a difficult river is not always a measure of your improvement. Instead, challenge yourself by making hard moves like ferries and surfing on easy rivers. All really good boaters develop their skills this way. Knowing your ability and matching it to appropriate rivers is the best way to ensure safe boating.

Preventable Risks in Whitewater Boating

On the first day of a beginner course, I remember standing thigh deep in Lake Fontana, gazing off at the southern tip of the Smoky Mountains, waiting patiently for the last student in my kayak class to paddle over for rolling instruction. The extra time it took him to drift to me provided clues to his fears. As I had guessed, he panicked when he finally let his boat flip upside down. "How do you feel?" I asked. "Okay," he muttered. "What's on your mind?" "Drowning," he admitted.

Gulp . . . as a professional instructor, I believe in insulating my students from unnecessary worry by teaching skills in a logical, reassuring progression. An outline of the day's activities, closely supervised wet exits, and maintaining a high regard for safety precautions usually serve this purpose. Unfortunately, this whitewater-bound beginner had arrived with fearful misconceptions about the safety of the sport. His well-meaning friends had sent him off with intimidating comments about his poor, ownerless dog starving. They had made teasing claims to his posthumous bank account. By the time he signed the purposefully graphic course waiver, my student's insecurities had overwhelmed him.

"Are you afraid of drowning here on the lake?" I asked. "No," he swallowed. "On the river then?" "Well . . . " he paused. "How many of the 150,000 people who travel the Nantahala each year do you think drown?" I asked, imagining the student's mind racing into the double digits. "Two drownings in 20 years." I explained, "Neither was a kayaker. One wasn't wearing a life jacket."

Immediately following this incident I described to the whole class the five preventable causes of death that give whitewater sports a risky reputation.

"Number one, alcohol is a common cause of accidents. That is clearly not an issue for us today. Number two, not wearing a tight-fitting PFD. Our class has already discussed this topic. Number three, no prior education in the sport contributes to 95 percent of whitewater accidents. Here we are in class, avoiding that mistake. Number four, flooded rivers are a frequent killer. Sadly, we are in the midst of a 5-year drought. Although we would welcome higher water, floods are certainly not a risk to us today. Number five, hypothermia. Clearly I am in the greatest danger, shivering slightly from 3 hours of roll instruction. You, however, are at no risk, basking in 90 degree temperatures with wet suits on." I noticed everyone's shoulders relax as I reviewed whitewater sports' five unnecessary killers. The class closed with smiles on everyone's face.

Paddler's River Hazards

The following river hazards are described briefly to help you to adapt an inquisitive attitude about river safety. The river sense of experienced boaters is based on cautiously evaluating rivers and rapids for potential threats.

Don't let these descriptions intimidate you. Your purpose is to understand the hazards clearly to know when they are a risk to your safety. For further explanation, ask local instructors to point hazards out on nearby rivers. In addition, the videos *Heads Up: River Rescue for River Runners, Uncalculated Risk,* and *Margin for Error* provide graphic examples of river hazards and rescue. The book *River Rescue* is another avenue to learn about the dynamics of whitewater accidents. See the appendix for more details.

Foot entrapment. Catching a foot in rocks on the bottom of the river can be caused by trying to stand up while getting swept downstream, usually in water midthigh to midtorso deep. Prevention is easy: stay in the safe swimmer's position (on your back, feet up and pointed downstream) unless the water is less than knee deep. Practice swimming on your back and maneuvering through rapids aggressively, looking between your feet at the side of the river you wish to avoid. In very deep water practice swimming freestyle on your stomach. River swimming wisdom is to ball up when swimming over a sheer drop of more than 3–4 feet (0.9–1.2 m).

Strainers. These are trees or single branches in the current with river water flowing through, which present a severe pinning hazard. Trees fall because of bank erosion, old age, floods, and storms. Look for strainers on wooded riverbanks, along small creeks after high water (often on the outside of a bend), and on less-frequented rivers. Assume they are present unless you know otherwise. Use downstream vision to spot bobbing twigs or irregular flow patterns.

Artificial entrapments. Anything artificial in the river is dangerous, a constant cause for alarm, and inherently more dangerous than most things natural. Keep an eye out for bridge pilings, low head dams, junked cars, and any other junk commonly found in urban riverways, under highway crossings, and at abandoned dam sites. Maintain a habit of visual downstream scanning. Avoid anything suspicious!

Broaches. This means getting pinned on a rock, either amidships or at one end. Avoid sharp rocks that can potentially crease a boat or that your kayak can be wrapped around. Lean into the rock with your boat and body tilting together like a bell buoy. Reach your body out to "love the rock"— touch it with your hand or paddle. Practice this skill with an instructor on gentle, shallow water until it becomes an instinct.

Strainers are one of the biggest dangers in whitewater.

Undercut rocks. Undercuts occur when a slab of rock or projecting rock shape forces the current to flow under the rock. Learn to spot them by the dark shadow on the upstream side of the rock, the lack of pillowing action by oncoming water, and the lack of a predictable eddy on the downstream side. Most dangerous undercuts are well known by locals and listed in guidebooks.

Entanglement. Getting tangled exiting your boat is most likely to be caused by ropes and loose lines in your boat. Practice wet exits and critically evaluate your outfitting for entanglement potential. Treat throw ropes as a potential hazard. Keep them neatly bagged, and carry a knife for rescue.

Vertical pins. These occur when the bow gets buried and pinned on the bottom after a steep drop. This is not a concern until you are paddling drops of over 3 or 4 feet (0.9–1.2 m). Advanced paddlers prevent them by checking the water depth first, and leaning back to keep the bow up. Paddling boats with large volume bows reduces this risk substantially, which is why creek boats have large volume!

Hydraulics. The worst hydraulics have evenly formed backwash with water moving back upstream for 4 feet (1.2 m) or more. Holes with more of a wave shape are intimidating but typically less hazardous than water flowing smoothly upstream. Dams, and hydraulics that are very regular, and perpendicular to the current are far more dangerous than hydraulics angled with one end downstream.

Long swims. Many people unfamiliar with the sport might expect long swims to be a primary killer. Since most beginning and intermediate rivers have pools between the drops, this is rarely the case. Wearing a tight PFD, matching your ability to an appropriate river, and being dressed for a swim can be excellent defenses against a long swim. Of course, another great precaution is a competent group of friends with either a shore- or boat-based rescue plan.

SAFETY TIP   Wear a helmet and learn to tuck tightly forward toward the deck when you flip. Dress appropriately for the water and air temperatures; dry suits or wet suits are a must if the combined water/air temperature is under 100 °F (38 °C).

Dealing With Fear

A common way to aggravate fears is by paddling with a group whose experience and interests in excitement are different from your own. My favorite example of this is a group of drill sergeants who were put up to a raft trip by their commander. The commander wanted guides to take the sergeants on a wild ride with a lot of risk. Understandably, when the drill sergeants arrived, few of them were looking forward to the trip in any way. The trip was, as a result, more conservative than most.

Sadly, the most common scenario of deepening fears is when a spouse or friend is dragged into the sport by an obviously more adventurous partner. In this situation, the reluctant companion often gets poorly fitting, hand-me-down equipment; less instruction; and less say in choosing river destinations. Paddle with people of similar skills and interests!

To deal with your river fears, remember that fear is a deeply ingrained protective mechanism. The horrible feeling you get is nothing more than extra energy for doing battle. Instead of considering yourself nervous, think of yourself as having extra energy. Treat your mind to images of running rapids successfully rather than dwelling on the worst that can happen.

Fear of whitewater is caused like any fear: Confusion and a lack of specific understanding allow your mind to manufacture anxiety and uneasiness. Identifying specific risks and choosing exactly where you paddle will go a long way toward harnessing your fears. Very few hazards are lurking in every rapid. Knowing when not to worry will undoubtedly make the sport more pleasant.

The difficulty of the water you paddle should match where you look and how far ahead you can read the water. Beginners tend to look only at the bow and slightly ahead. Intermediates tend to see eddies along the shore and look well down the rapid. Expert paddlers catch eddies while scanning downstream for hazards and upstream for other boaters. Developing your scanning patterns will actually improve your skill level.

Whitewater Classifications

The whitewater river rating system classifies rivers as Class I to Class VI, from easiest to most difficult. While the system is a useful guide, to get an accurate idea of the difficulty of a run you need to get a full description. This will include information about the nature of the rapids. Do they alternate between drops and pools or are they continuous? What is the gradient? What is the volume? How many major rapids are there, and are they easily portaged? Is the river generally thought to be safe or dangerous?

This system is not exact. Rivers do not easily fit into one category, and regional or individual interpretations may cause misunderstandings. Allow an extra margin for safety when the water is cold or if the river is remote.

Class I: Easy. Fast moving water with riffles and small waves. Few obstructions, all obvious and avoided with little training. Risk to swimmers is slight, self-rescue is easy.

Class II: Novice. Straightforward rapids with wide, clear channels that are evident without scouting. Occasional maneuvering may be required, but rocks and medium-sized waves are easily avoided by trained paddlers. Swimmers are seldom injured, and group assistance, while helpful, is seldom needed.

Class III: Intermediate. Rapids with moderate, irregular waves that may be difficult to avoid and that can swamp an open canoe. Complex maneuvers in fast current and good boat control in tight passages or around ledges is often required. Large waves or strainers may be present but can be easily avoided. Strong eddies and powerful current effects can be found, particularly on large volume rivers. Scouting is advisable for inexperienced parties. Injuries while swimming are rare; self-rescue is usually easy, but group assistance may be required to avoid long swims.

Class IV: Advanced. Intense, powerful, but predictable rapids requiring precise boat handling in turbulent water. Depending on the character of the river it may feature large, unavoidable waves and holes or constricted passages demanding fast maneuvers under pressure. A fast, reliable eddy turn may be required to initiate maneuvers, scout rapids, or rest. Rapids may require "must" moves upstream of dangerous hazards. Scouting is necessary the first time down. Risk of injury to swimmers is moderate to high,

Serious Class V–VI whitewater—recommended for experts only.

and water conditions make self-rescue difficult. Group assistance for rescue is often essential and requires practiced skills. A strong roll is highly recommended.

Class V: Expert. Extremely long, obstructed, or very violent rapids that expose a paddler to above average endangerment. Drops may contain large, unavoidable waves and holes or steep, congested chutes with complex, demanding routes. Rapids may continue for long distances between pools, demanding a high level of fitness. What eddies exist may be small, turbulent, and difficult to reach. Scouting is mandatory, but often difficult. Swims are dangerous, and rescue is difficult even for experts. A very reliable roll, proper equipment, extensive experience, and practiced rescue skills are essential for survival.

Class VI: Extreme. These runs often exemplify the extremes of difficulty, unpredictability, and danger. The consequences of errors are severe and rescue may be impossible. For teams of experts only, at favorable water levels, after close inspection and taking all precautions. This class does not include drops thought to be unrunnable, but may include drops only occasionally run.

Reading Just Isn't Enough

Many of the skills discussed in this chapter require experience to apply, so simply reading about them is only the first step of your learning process. Whitewater kayakers need more than just good boat control—they need well-practiced techniques for dealing with whitewater conditions. Learning kayaking requires a careful learning progression, best established by an experienced instructor in your area. If you try to bite off too difficult or too long a trip, you really rob yourself of the opportunity to learn and progress safely. Start with short journeys with experienced friends to ensure an enjoyable experience in kayaking.

5

SEA KAYAKING TECHNIQUES AND SAFETY

Sea kayaks can take you to your dreams. . . to a secluded, unexplored island; to view an eagle's nest; to paddle around with dolphins. Whatever your destination, particularly in large lakes or the ocean, you'll need a set of techniques to keep you safe and to keep the trip pleasurable.

Whitewater kayakers can skip this chapter, unless they plan on heading to the ocean for surfing or tours.

Launching

A well-protected launch zone is the best situation for beginners starting an outing. Look for protection in a small bay where the waves don't crash in. Most public launch areas are in protected bays, easily accessible even at low tide. Private land and limited public access complicate the start of a trip in many regions.

When waves characterize the only launch site available, launching a sea kayak in swells can be the most challenging portion of a day trip. Trying to put on the spray skirt and paddle out with some speed before the next wave crashes on shore is not easy for the beginning paddler. The easiest system involves having experienced paddlers help launch most of the group, and launching themselves last.

Regardless of wave conditions, learn to anticipate wave patterns and sets. Watch how frequently the large waves approach, and see if there is a pattern to when the smallest waves come in. Predicting wave size and pattern will be useful in landings as well.

Paddling hard is the key to launching through the surf zone.

Understanding the Tides and Currents

As the tide rises and falls, large volumes of water are redistributed in the sea. The currents that move this water can be quite strong and can make returning to shore unexpectedly difficult, often taking you farther than you planned. Occasionally, an ebbing (going out) tide can pose a severe threat from the speed and power it has to carry you from shore.

Tidal current tables, different from charts that show simple high and low tides, provide detailed information on water currents and are available in many coastal areas. Some tables are voluminous, such as those for the Pacific Northwest that show widely varied currents between the network of islands found there. Along other, less-featured coastlines, tidal currents can be summarized in a table of only a few pages.

This information can be critical to a kayaker. For instance, imagine that you are planning an 8-mile (13-km) journey south along the coast. If you paddle continuously, you might average 3–4 miles per hour (5–6.5 kph); therefore, you should figure on 2.5 hours for the journey if there is no current.

However, upon checking the tidal current tables you realize that if you were to leave at your typical launching time of noon, you would be battling a 3-mph (5-kph) headcurrent and would barely be making any progress. An early 7 a.m. start, on the other hand, could have you paddling with a 2-mph (3-kph) current assist, cutting your time considerably. This could leave you time to lounge around or explore your destination before catching the afternoon current back to your launch site.

Be sure to check tidal current tables before setting up camp to avoid getting waterlogged during your stay.

Tide changes can have a dramatic effect on the difficulty of paddling in other ways. Sometimes a low tide leaves a shallow area exposed, making for a much longer return trip or a nasty slog through mud flats. Tides complicate timing the length of a day trip. Usually, locations where this is true are well known by local paddlers and clearly marked on charts.

More than one camp set-up or lunch stop has been unexpectedly swamped by an overlooked tide. For instance, in Maine the tidal change can be up to 15 feet (4.6 m), wreaking havoc on the unprepared. However, this is easy to avoid, since coastal communities have readily accessible tide tables that indicate high and low tide as well as the variations to be expected. Experienced local paddlers can be a great source of information on the area's currents and tides.

Landing

Finishing the trip in surf can pose a real challenge for you and your equipment. As with launchings, a carefully chosen, protected area can make the task much easier. Search for shallow beaches or pebble beaches hidden in rocky shores. When forced to do a surf landing, find a small set of waves and time your final sprint to cover the most distance between waves. You'll use a stop-and-go cadence to allow waves to pass under you before they start to curl. A friend on shore, ready to help stabilize your quick exit, can make the landing a lot easier.

If you haven't used good timing to avoid the waves during a landing, their curling, crashing crests will quickly turn you sideways. Riding the wave in sideways is an option but requires an excellent brace and lean into the wave (away from the beach). Surf kayakers thrive on the excitement of this ride, particularly in shorter, highly maneuverable boats. For most sea kayakers, it is extra excitement that is not always appreciated.

Returning to shore in the Sea of Cortez, Mexico.

Navigating

Nautical charts are a must for long day trips and any open water crossings. They can be fun to use on short day trips. Your first trips are likely to be in areas with islands and low-relief, featureless coastlines, so unless you know the area very well these charts are a good thing to have and use. For some regions and trips, you might want the additional land relief and features provided by a topographical (topo) map.

Get the most detailed scale available and a chart case to keep the map protected but accessible. Charts show navigational buoys, as well as low tide designations to indicate which ledges will be apparent. Add to the adventure of a short trip by checking your progress on a group tour. This is the best way to safely learn navigational skills.

With a compass, orient your nautical chart to magnetic north, and mark your desired path on your chart. Then, by moving the compass along your

Using a compass and chart to plan a trip.

marked course, calculate what bearing you will have to follow. Calculate how long the trip should take, and be sure to factor in tidal currents, wind, and your average paddling speed.

Strong currents in channel crossings require special strategies to maintain the bearing and time required to get to your destination. In short crossings, keeping the boat angled slightly into the current will allow a continuous movement forward. This *ferry angle* is borrowed from the old riverboat ferries' means of propulsion across the river. Another option is to depart well upstream of the destination, allowing the current to bring you downstream.

Some of the sea kayaking books listed in the appendix have special sections on using bearings, landmarks, and triangulation. These are important skills for all but the easiest of day tours.

Every region has its own traits and hazards that only experienced paddlers recognize. Be prepared for them by checking with local shops and outfitters for an appraisal of local conditions. Find out about the kind of currents to expect in channel crossings, the navigational rules for dealing with other vessels, the tidal patterns, and local weather patterns. Local guidebooks identify hazardous tidal rips, as well as notoriously windy and dangerous points.

Reading the Weather

Remember "Red sky at night, sailor's delight; red sky at morn, sailors be warned"? Understanding weather forecasts and developing basic prediction skills are crucial to safe paddling on open water. The safest paddling is generally in the morning, before winds begin to come up. Often coastal areas are choppy in the afternoon. Fog can be a real hazard, especially on warm summer days over a cold sea. In these situations, everyone in your group should know a compass heading that will get them back to land. In addition, having whistles can help with regrouping.

Since the sea kayak is the smallest craft on the water, it is the most sensitive to the weather—especially to the wind. Frontal patterns in the clouds can give immediate feedback on advancing weather, particularly when combined with knowledge about regional weather patterns. A barometer also indicates weather changes. Practice studying weather patterns before your first big trip! Many kayakers take along weather radios on trips in order to hear advisories and basic forecasts.

Wind

Wind causes two problems for the kayaker. First, a wind coming from any direction (except head on) tends to make the boat spin around and sweep it sideways. Not only does this throw the boater off course, it makes the kayak feel less stable. Winds from any direction make paddling and judging the time required to cover a certain distance very difficult.

Tail winds can be a paddler's friend as long as the winds continue directly along your route; however, if they are at even a slight angle, they can become a difficult obstacle. Winds over 10 knots (12 mph, 19 kph) make paddling too difficult for the beginner, even with an easy to access landing beach. Directional control is lost, and the waves generated by wind create another hazard. Winds of 10 to 15 knots can be identified by the size of the waves they make, 1 to 1-1/2 feet (30–46 cm) tall. The longer the fetch, or distance the waves have been building, the more severe the waves will be.

RULES OF THE SEA

When paddling in areas with other traffic, particularly around large boats, assume they can't see you. Not only is a sea kayak smaller than most other craft, but normal conditions like glare can hide a boat from easy view. Some paddlers use an orange flag on a tall, flexible pole, the type bicyclists use for visibility. Still, the best defense is a carefully planned trip to avoid areas and times of high traffic.

Motorized craft yield to sailboats, which in turn yield to boats under manual power. However, this doesn't give sea kayakers exemption from the basic rules:

- Vessels keep to the right in narrow passages.

- Vessels limited to a channel may not be hampered in transit by other, smaller traffic. Particularly when crossing commercial shipping lanes, kayakers should be extra cautious and prompt.

- Ideally, trips should be planned to avoid highly congested areas.

Sea Kayaking Safety

Sea kayaking may seem more benign than whitewater boating, but don't let appearances fool you. Sea kayaking has its own hazards. You must learn how to read charts and maps, anticipate tides and their resulting effects, and anticipate changes in weather. Practicing those skills is the best way to remain safe on the sea. Other safety issues include knowing how to deal with ocean traffic, being prepared for unexpected weather, and knowing what to do if you're caught by nightfall.

Paddling at sunset is a great way to end the day's activities, but night paddling should be avoided unless you're highly skilled and properly equipped.

Dealing With Weather

Even with careful planning and attention to weather forecasts, an unexpected storm is likely to catch you sometime in your paddling career. Have alternate plans for landings and be very certain that storms are unlikely before you plan major crossings. Keeping your group together and knowing rescues can improve your ability to weather the storm. Having a two-way radio or cellular phone can simplify a rescue situation.

Night Paddling

Night paddling, while offering special rewards, should be avoided, unless your boat is equipped with appropriate running lights and you are equipped with well-practiced navigational skills. Nonetheless, long day trips should include nighttime signaling devices for emergency use. Consult your local outfitter for recommendations for specific styles.

Signaling Devices

Sea kayakers should always carry signaling devices. They are needed to attract the attention of group members or other craft, to avoid a collision, or to signal for assistance or a rescue.

Hand-held and aerial flares, strobes, and orange smoke canisters are the simplest and most common devices for attracting attention. A whistle or foghorn can be used within a group, but neither is likely to be heard by motorized craft. Waterproof flashlights provide a small margin of safety in the event that your return trip is delayed until after dark. The marine environment is harsh on equipment, so take back-up signaling devices to be safe. With recent advances in technology, two-way VHF radios and cellular phones are rapidly becoming the first line of communication for sea kayakers.

Rescues

Despite the best laid plans, sea kayak paddlers sometimes require a rescue of some sort. If you capsize and have to leave the boat, you should do a wet exit (see pp. 35–36). Every paddler should know and practice capsize recovery systems to get back in the boat, but it's also important for a group to be well practiced in rescue skills so they can successfully assist paddlers in trouble. There are zillions of rescues that work, and everyone has their favorites. We are going to cover some of the most basic and effective rescues.

As a kayaker, you will want to know reliable rescues so you can minimize your exposure to the elements. Each rescue is designed to get you back into the safety of your boat so you can paddle away in a comfortable, stable manner. In most cases, taking a swim is no big deal if you are well practiced at options and prepared for the water. The temperature of oceans and lakes can be a frigid 40 °F (4 °C), enough to shock you initially and rob you of your strength after a few minutes of immersion. It's wise to dress for the water temperature in case of an unexpected swim.

Assisted Rescue

The importance of paddling in a group can't be overemphasized. A group of paddlers well practiced in rescue skills can deal successfully with many threatening conditions.

First, know that starting the trip with a group isn't enough to keep you safe. Paddlers travel at different speeds as the natural outcome of their varying skills and interests. However, before the trip, every member should commit to reuniting with the group at specified stops along the way. Buddy systems, where a novice paddler is paired with a veteran of the sport, are especially helpful. Some groups work well with a trip leader who is familiar with the area along with a sweep boat to follow at the end. Stay within communication distance of your companions. Just for fun, do a wet exit and try climbing back into your boat with no assistance. This will quickly make you understand the benefits of paddling in a group. In any rescue, it is especially important to hang on to your gear to prevent winds from blowing it out of reach.

Raft, Reenter, and Pump

The most common assisted rescue is when the rescuing paddler rafts up to, or pulls alongside, the swamped boat to stabilize it for reentry. Rescuers should always assert themselves with clear directions for the swimmer to help expedite the rescue process.

Once rafted up, a paddle can span the kayaks. The rescuer leans over and grabs the cockpit to provide stability. Paddlers position the kayaks side-by-side in the bow-to-stern stabilizing position, the basic position used for gaining the stability needed for reentry and to pump out water. The swimmer reenters with a hard kick to lunge his chest over the stern deck. Then pump the water out. After the water is removed, the swimmer can reenter the kayak. Anytime a paddler has trouble reentering the boat, a 6-foot (1.8-m) stirrup made from a loop of rope or webbing can be hung from the paddle to provide a welcome step to ease reentry.

T Rescue

There is an alternative to all this pumping. In the T rescue, the rescuer moves perpendicular to the swamped boat. The rescuer lifts the bow while the swimmer pushes down on the stern. They flip the boat and pull it into the bow-to-stern stabilizing position. This is a quick and efficient way to get the paddler back in a dry boat.

TX Rescue

The TX rescue is used when the swamped boat has no bulkheads to form watertight compartments. This rescue is performed like a T rescue except the swamped boat is pulled farther over the rescuer's deck to drain it completely. This requires a lot of teamwork and effort.

Tandem Boat Assisted Rescue

Rescues of tandem boats are modified slightly. In using the T rescue for a tandem boat, two paddlers can stabilize each other to provide the support necessary for lifting the swamped boat and emptying the water.

Towing

Though not technically a rescue technique, towing systems are handy in group situations when one paddler is sick or simply runs out of energy. Use sturdy lines that can be quickly released.

Self-Rescue

If you're out of reach of other paddlers, you'll have to know how to rescue yourself. Self-rescues are much harder than assisted rescues. Getting the water out of a capsized boat and getting back into the boat by yourself are tricky. Having a pump to bail water out of your boat after a flip is essential, especially if you are paddling on your own.

Paddle Float

One of the most important capsize recovery systems uses a paddle float as an outrigger. This works reliably in calm water without outside assistance, but paddlers debate its effectiveness in rough conditions. You will need a float to attach to the end of your paddle. This rescue is easiest if your kayak has deck rigging to hold the paddle float in position as an outrigger.

A paddle float acts as an outrigger to stabilize the boat for reentry.

After the swim, hang onto the boat with a leg in the cockpit. This frees both hands to attach the paddle float to the blade and inflate it if necessary. Then flip the boat upright and position the paddle into the rigging perpendicularly so it can work as an outrigger. Next kick with your legs to spread your body out flat on the water before lunging your chest onto the stern deck. Slide one leg into the cockpit, then the other. Then turn toward the paddle float to establish a sitting position. These steps keep your center of gravity low throughout the rescue to avoid flipping. At this point, a bilge pump can empty the water from your boat so you can continue on your way.

If you don't have rigging, position the paddle shaft behind the cockpit rim so your hand can grasp both the paddle shaft and cockpit rim. Once your chest is up over the stern, reposition your hands to maintain the paddle float support.

A stirrup to assist your reentry to the boat is an option. A paddle float made of foam is the preference of paddlers in very cold regions, where cold hands and shock prevent efficient inflating.

Practice Rescues

You should know and practice a full repertoire of rescues and be prepared for the initial shock of hitting the cold water. Practice in warm water under calm conditions, so you will gain confidence in your rescue ability. Take a class to learn some of the finer points of rescues and to get valuable feedback on your form. It's harder than it sounds, so don't even think that you know all you need to know from simply reading and looking at the pictures!

Reading Just Isn't Enough

Many of the skills discussed in this chapter require experience to apply, so simply reading about them is only the first step of your learning process. Sea kayakers need more than just good boat control—they need well-practiced techniques for dealing with river and sea conditions. Learning sea kayaking requires a careful learning progression, best established by an experienced instructor in your area. If you try to bite off too difficult or too long a trip, you really rob yourself of the opportunity to learn and progress safely. Start with short journeys with experienced friends to ensure an enjoyable experience in kayaking.

6

THE BEST PLACES TO KAYAK

Kayaking opens up an entire world of places to visit and explore. Each river, bay, and lake has its own personality. Every time you paddle your kayak, you get to know that water's personality, play with it, work with it, just as you would a person.

Planning a Trip

Planning short day trips can be as easy as checking with a local outfitter for suggested destinations. Calculating the distance to travel and the time allowed can be an acquired skill. Talk to others who've made the trip to figure out how much time is needed. Or look in paddling books that describe the area and trips in it.

Beginning sea kayak paddlers usually start with shorter trips, in an organized group. Choose sheltered coastal regions with lots of islands and bays for wind protection. Longer sea kayaking trips involve reading charts and establishing routes and bearings. These trips require a compass, either hand-held or the more expensive and convenient deck-mounted variety. Maps of the area and charts that include your intended route are a must for all but the shortest day trips. Plan to paddle out with an outgoing tidal current and return with an incoming tidal current for an easier trip.

Just as pilots file a flight plan, both whitewater and sea paddlers should describe their outing to a friend who knows their skills, destination, and timetable. With this information, assistance can be mobilized in a more organized manner if necessary.

Taking Off

You'll probably drive to most launch destinations, but should you want to get somewhere far enough away to make air travel attractive, it's good to know that traveling by airplane with kayaks is possible, though flying with whitewater kayaks is considerably easier than toting sea kayaks. At 10 to 12 feet (3.0–3.7 m), whitewater boats fit in any commercial jet, while sea kayaks will only fit in a few planes. In my experience, getting prior approval from an airline is very difficult, except for on-the-ball airlines that list kayaks with other sporting goods. Kayaks don't fit commuter airlines' propeller planes, so plan your trip accordingly. An itinerary that doesn't require changing planes is best. Expect to pay from $75 to $200 as a fee for excess baggage, or from $200 to $600 if you are successfully referred to air cargo. Needless to say, checking your boat as excess baggage is nearly always preferable, unless you want the insurance coverage and predictability of air cargo service.

Expect the unexpected! Sometimes you'll walk up to the airline counter with your boat and be greeted by a warm smile and no charge for the boat. Other times, the ticket agent will proclaim "That won't fit." When this roadblock comes at the start of your trip, simply ask for the manager and plead your case with a big smile. If it happens on your return trip, that's when you scramble to find the baggage claim receipt from your trip out. If you plan a lot of airline travel with a boat you might consider an inflatable or folding kayak!

Foreign paddling can be a great experience, but probably you'll want your first kayak trip to be a fairly controlled experience, possibly with a commercial outfitter. Relying on an outfitter will save you the major hassles of boat rental and transport. Limitless adventure travel opportunities exist around the world, but be forewarned that the combination of foreign travel and kayaking leads to adventure that is not always controllable. Sometimes the river floods or the ocean storms, putting a damper on any trip. If you take an adventure trip, make a commitment to have fun no matter what transpires. This will help guarantee a wonderful experience.

Lingo and difficulty ratings do vary internationally. In much of the world, paddle sports are generically called *canoesport* (*kanusport* in German-influenced regions), but the boat is still called a kayak. British paddlers replace the terms *peel-outs* and *eddy turns* with *break-ins* and *break-outs*. New Zealanders are notorious for underrating their rivers, so if you paddle there, pick an easy river for starters!

Mind Your Manners

Wherever you go, there are environmental and social responsibilities for kayakers. On whitewater rivers, you should be especially courteous to fishermen and avoid them wherever possible. Be sensitive to the rights and privacy of landowners and neighboring townsfolk. Different regions vary in their acceptance of outsiders and the weird dress of kayakers.

It's important to mind your manners wherever you paddle.

On the sea as well as on inland lakes, the booming numbers of kayakers are adding a strain to fragile shorelines. Use existing approved camps and fire pits whenever possible. Otherwise, get permission to camp and leave no trace by using stoves and fire pans. Respect the regional requirements for sanitation, since you'll often be in the watershed or tidal zone. (An increasing number of locations, particularly rivers in the western U.S., enforce a strict carry-out policy.) Avoid contaminating freshwater stream heads with any—even biodegradable—soaps. Steer clear of rookeries where you might disturb feeding patterns of birds or other animals. A good rule of thumb is to stay far enough away that you don't cause a change in their behavior.

Family Affair

I was really a pretty lucky kid. My parents started me paddling when I was about 15 years old. They had done a little bit of backpacking, had seen kayakers out on the river, and thought, "Let's try it!" They started with a C-2, a decked-over canoe. My dad stuck me up in the front of that boat and dragged me off on weekends. I simply filled the front cockpit of the boat

Paddling is the perfect sport for the entire family.

while my dad tried to spark my interest in paddling; I would have preferred watching football games. But after I learned a little boat control, and especially as I met other kids my age out doing the sport, I began to look forward to my weekend on the water. When I turned 16, my driver's license and the family car gave me the freedom to get caught up in the world of kayaking.

Kayaking can be a family sport. I remember years of summer vacations with our family all loaded in the car, heading off to a river for boating, exploring, and hiking around. Now, 20 years later, we have our annual family reunion on a river somewhere in the U.S. Typically, we pick a 2-week, easy western whitewater trip where we carry all of our gear on rafts. It's rare to find a sport that's such a perfect lifetime family activity.

Children should be at least 7 years old before they go on their own in a boat. Their first solo trip should be very controlled to avoid any chance of a threatening experience that could turn them off to kayaking forever. Kids 10 to 15 can really thrive in the sport and learn it very quickly. As with any activity, though, kids have less sense of responsibility and overall safety. Very young children can go on short sea kayaking tours in a tandem boat, especially when the trip is in a protected area with easy exit options.

United States Waterways

One way to get more information about kayaking in your area is to go to a popular paddling destination. These are good places to watch other paddlers and get suggestions on where to learn.

In most regions, local outfitters offer classes or tours that are a good way to get introduced to the waterways of the area. You can learn about the difficulty and specific hazards of various local trips. The appendix lists a few regional shops that can help get you started. You might be able to check out some of these places and talk to the local paddlers to get their recommendations on where to learn more.

SAFETY TIP Only a few of the following rivers and waterways mentioned are recommended for beginner paddlers. Popular intermediate and advanced destinations are described since they are fun places to watch and ask questions about paddling.

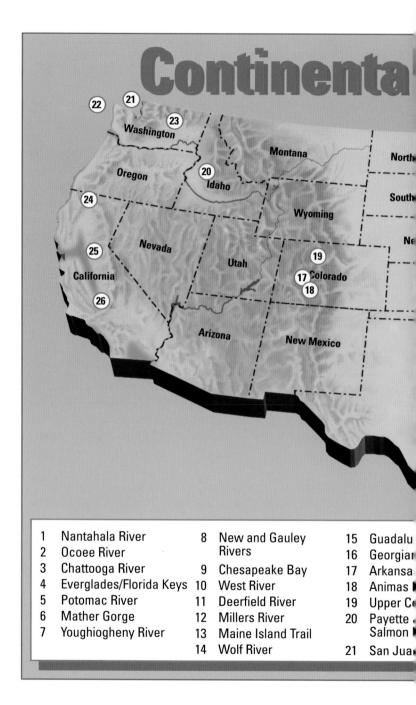

Continenta

SOUTHEAST

Nantahala River, near Bryson City, North Carolina, is the undisputed beginners' destination of the Southeast. The 8-mile (13-km) stretch of continuous Class II whitewater ends in Nantahala Falls, a good Class III climax to the trip. Nantahala Outdoor Center (my place of work for 13 years) boasts the nation's largest whitewater school and a collection of some of the finest instructors.

The Ocoee River (Ducktown, Tennessee) is a very popular and playful 4-mile (6.4-km) run of Class III–IV whitewater. Perhaps the most densely traveled whitewater river in the world, the Ocoee gets over 225,000 visitors annually by raft, canoe, and kayak. Water levels are controlled year round by the Tennessee Valley Authority (TVA), a government agency that has found it more profitable to release water from dams for recreation than for power generation. The upstream portion of the Ocoee will host the 1996 Olympic Slalom event. The Chattooga (Clayton, Georgia) offers a southeastern paddler refuge from the crowds. A federally designated "Wild and Scenic River," the Chattooga is remote, difficult, and, with its technical rapids and wildly varying water levels, potentially dangerous.

From Charleston to Savannah, GA, the coastline offers surprising scenery and wildlife, including the frequent opportunity to play with dolphins. Dolphins circle your boat in curiosity, often accompanying you on your paddle.

The warm and shallow lakes, inlets, and coasts of Florida make it a popular destination for sea kayaking. Exploring the Everglades and less populated islands of the Florida Keys rewards you with a rich variety of seabirds, marine animals, and opportunities for observing nature.

© F-Stock/Greg Lashbrook

The islands of the Florida Keys provide a great setting for kayaking and nature-watching.

EAST CENTRAL STATES

The Potomac River, near Washington, DC, is a fine example of a spectacular river very close to a metropolitan area. Mather Gorge, just below Great Falls (Maryland and Virginia), is a good learning site at appropriate water levels, yet offers thrills for even the wildest expert. In late summer, very early in the morning, you might be able to see these expert paddlers running the spout of Great Falls, a 33-foot (10-m) drop.

The headwaters of the Potomac have several popular stretches of whitewater, and also plenty of less popular, but delightful, secret places to explore. The Youghiogheny (Ohiopyle, Pennsylvania) is a very popular Class II–III run, with several excellent paddling schools in the area. In the mountain state of West Virginia, the New and Gauley rivers are very popular among advanced paddlers and rafters.

Sea kayaking is growing in popularity on the upper reaches of Chesapeake Bay. This is home to one of the nation's leading sea kayaking symposia.

NEW ENGLAND STATES

No single river stands out as the most popular area for paddling in the Northeast. The West River (Jamaica, Vermont) has fall water releases from the power plant along two sections: a short Class IV section, and an easier Class II stretch downstream. In Massachusetts, check out Zoar Gap on the Deerfield River, or Millers Falls on the Millers. Both have excellent whitewater schools nearby. Northeast boaters pray for rainfall in the dry part of summer or fall, since that opens up hundreds of delightful rivers.

Sea kayaking is ideal along all the less-populated stretches of the northeastern coast, with the most popular destinations clustered in Maine. The Maine Island Trail winds its way among 3,000 islands, with camping allowed on many for easy trip-planning options. Well-prepared adventurers can venture farther up the Bay of Fundy and explore the Fundy Isles and the other shores of New Brunswick (see Canada's map on pages 98-99).

CENTRAL STATES FROM TEXAS TO WISCONSIN

Paddlers from the coasts like to joke about how far these Midwestern paddlers will drive to get on mountain rivers. For some, 12-hour drives each way are common for a weekend of paddling! Central paddlers counter that they are closer to the best paddling of both the Rocky and Appalachian mountains. What they won't tell you are the names of their perfectly excellent local rivers like the Wolf River in Wisconsin or the Guadalupe near San Antonio, Texas.

It isn't exactly a sea, but the northern shore of Lake Superior offers delightful sea (coastal) kayaking. Stop by your local video rental store and check out Bill Mason's *Waterwalker,* a delightful, artistic look at exploring these shores by canoe. Visit the Georgian Bay on Lake Huron and the shores of Michigan's Upper Peninsula. The boundary waters of Minnesota and the adjacent Quetico Provincial Park in Canada (see Canada's map) are famous for canoe expeditions, and kayaks are welcome in the Land of 10,000 Lakes. Several million acres of rugged terrain are accessible only by self-propelled watercraft.

ROCKY MOUNTAINS
The Arkansas River near Buena Vista, Colorado, offers more miles of Class III–IV whitewater than any other river in the continental United States. Dropping through Colorado from the back side of the Aspen and Vail ski resorts, the "Ark" has cold but thrilling water and some excellent whitewater schools and rafting companies.

The Animas, in Durango, CO, offers perhaps the best downtown whitewater of any U.S. river, and a very fine school. There is lots of paddling throughout the Rockies: the upper Colorado River and tributaries, and the Payette and Salmon rivers near McCall, Idaho. The beautiful rivers of Montana are gaining worldwide respect. The West offers plenty of multiday trips in awesome canyons (permits are required).

Doing an "ender" on the Piedra River, Colorado.

Sea kayaking is possible on local lakes or along coastlines accessed by long car rides. Paddlers in the southern Rockies often head through Mexico to Baja, while paddlers in the northern areas find the Pacific Northwest more accessible.

NORTHWEST

The entire Northwest coast has more sea kayaks and sea kayak schools than anywhere in the world and is home to the world's sea kayaking capital, Seattle, Washington. A number of Seattle-area residents use their kayaks for transportation and as a source of exercise. Exploring the coastlines of the San Juan Islands is the focus of most weekend trips. Watching the whales and orcas is, for many, the highlight of sea kayaking anywhere. Nowhere is sea kayaking more popular than around Barkley Sound and the Queen Charlotte Islands. Southeastern Alaska is one of the premiere places in the world to sea kayak among the glaciers.

Whitewater runs are common in the mountains. Perhaps most popular are the Wenatchee and the Klamath rivers.

CALIFORNIA

The South Fork of the American River near Placerville, California, offers good, clean Class III whitewater drops through the region that was the heart of the 1800s California Gold Rush. Floating down the river, it is common to come upon modern-day prospectors looking for the elusive mother lode. Paddlers wait until later in the day during a dry summer to catch the full flow of the dam release.

Anywhere you go in the Sierras, there are ski areas with literally tons of wet snow at high elevations. That is a prescription for excellent runoff and lots of migrant outdoor sports workers looking for rivers to run for work and pleasure. A Southern California whitewater classic is on the Kern River near Kernville.

If you keep going south, into Mexico, you'll find Baja California's coastline is second only to the state of Washington in sea kayaking popularity. My own experience there was a tandem boat adventure to Isla Tiburón for several days of camping, diving, and exploration. Only after we arrived on the island did I glean that tiburón means shark in Spanish. We enjoyed a delightful trip, encountering no sharks and seeing no other people.

Canada

Just north of Calgary and running through Banff and Jasper is the Kananaskis River. The "Kan" features a 1.6-kilometer (1-mi) enhanced rapid, with

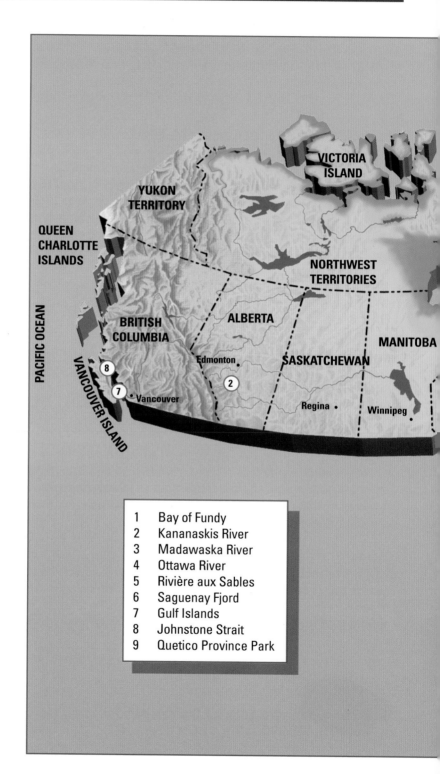

1	Bay of Fundy
2	Kananaskis River
3	Madawaska River
4	Ottawa River
5	Rivière aux Sables
6	Saguenay Fjord
7	Gulf Islands
8	Johnstone Strait
9	Quetico Province Park

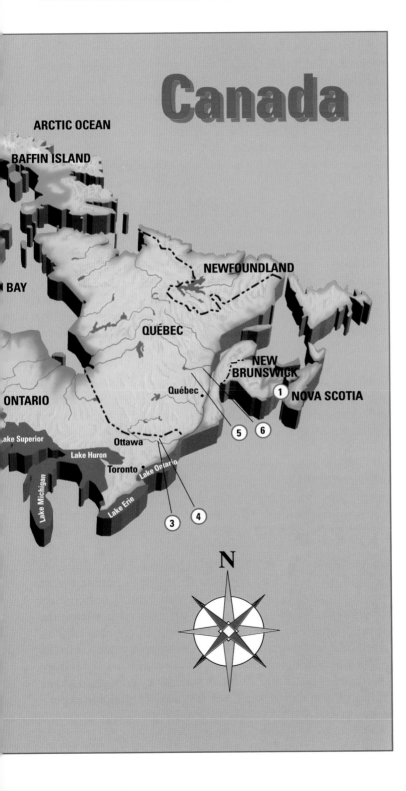

Canada

ARCTIC OCEAN

BAFFIN ISLAND

BAY

NEWFOUNDLAND

QUÉBEC

NEW
BRUNSWICK

ONTARIO

Québec

NOVA SCOTIA

1

5   6

Lake Superior

Ottawa

Lake Huron

Toronto

Lake Ontario

Lake Michigan

Lake Erie

3   4

N

different sections appropriate for all levels of paddlers. To enhance the rapid, paddlers supervised some bulldozer rearranging of rocks to organize eddies and play waves. The site is occasional host to play-boating rodeos and slalom events, including the Canadian National Championships.

In Ontario, the undisputed beginners' river is the Madawaska, home of Madawaska Kanu Camp of Barry's Bay. MKC is one of the premiere schools in North America, largely because of the warm, dam-controlled, unpolluted, and uncrowded whitewater. A 6.4-kilometer (4-mi) section offers beginners opportunities, as well as play holes for advanced paddlers. Check with MKC before you go to confirm water release schedules.

Just north of MKC is the Ottawa River, one of the most popular rafting rivers in Canada. The huge volume of the Ottawa (often over 300 m³/s or 10,000 cfs), combined with a spectacular wilderness setting, make this a pretty awe-inspiring run. You would probably want your first descent to be by commercial raft trip.

Québec has dammed many of its rivers to sell power to the United States, yet they still seem to have quite a few raging whitewater runs. Perhaps most notable is the Rivière aux Sables, near Jonquière. This site of the 1979 World Championships has several sections of varied difficulty a short drive from the race site, which now hosts an outdoor center and whitewater school.

A frequent sea kayaker's destination in Québec is the Saguenay Fjord. One of the largest, longest, and southernmost fjords in the northern hemisphere, the Saguenay shelters several arctic animals in its cold, deep waters, and is protected by a narrow mouth to the Atlantic. The fjord features cliffs towering more than 300 meters (1,000 ft) over the water. Whales and seals are a frequent sight. The fjord starts near Chicoutimi and reaches 97 kilometers (60 mi) north and east to the Atlantic. The entire trip can take 5 or more days, but many take advantage of easy access from nearby towns and opt for day trips. Trips should be carefully planned for safety measures; the cold water, tidal currents, and steep walls complicate escape options.

The best-known sea kayaking in Canada is along the west coast. The Gulf Islands, on the leeward side of Vancouver Island, British Columbia, are an excellent and magical example of the wildlife and sculpted shorelines accessible only by kayak. On the northern end of Vancouver Island, the Johnstone Strait is perhaps the best place in the world to see orca whales, commonly referred to as killer whales. The large currents common in the many narrow inlets and channels help create a very rich marine environment, which is believed to attract the orcas. People lucky enough to kayak in their vicinity, listening and observing, say it is an unforgettable experience. It's on my to-do list!

England and Scotland

Nestled in Nottingham is a concrete-lined artificial whitewater racecourse. While the course offers challenges sufficient for world competitions, it also has sections that are ideal for beginners. The lake just upstream is ideal for classes and stroke practice. Since the river is dam controlled, the water is frequently available to both recreational paddlers and Britain's national team. Since the water is guaranteed, many paddlers simply head for Nottingham.

Kayaking access to rivers in Britain is very limited because very powerful fishing clubs control access. Canals that run throughout the majority of mainland Britain get a lot of kayak traffic. Since the canals were the transportation infrastructure, many weave scenic routes through cities. Canal societies are revamping some of the older canals and making them accessible for tourism and local recreation. Canals provide an excellent way to see England. Many towns host active paddling clubs; in fact, there are several along the River Thames, including one in the shadow of Windsor Castle.

For many river trips in England, you have to wait until the day after it rains for enough water. But it rains quite a bit in England, so rivers seem to run in 15-hour cycles. The Brathy, Tees, Tyne, and Esk rivers are commonly run whitewater sections requiring good rains. The Eden River near Kendall has more consistent flows, as does the Leven, which, for reasons unknown to the author, may only be run on the fourth Sunday of the month.

The River Tryeryn near Bala and Llangothlin, in northern Wales, is a popular intermediate trip. Although dam released, this river is small volume, almost creeklike, and winds its way toward the town of Bala and the confluence of the River Dee. The River Dee flows through the town of Llangothlin, offering a 3-kilometer (2-mi) stretch of Class III/IV whitewater. Above the take-out from the river, there is a canal that allows paddling back up to the put-in to run another descent. Both Bala and Llangothlin have paddling centers for instruction. While visiting the area, you'll also find Plas Y Brenin, a big outdoor center with lots of shops, people, and activity, is also worth a visit.

In Scotland, the River Tay is the most popular whitewater trip. The difficulty varies with the water level, so the river entertains a wide variety of paddlers. Scotland has more liberal access laws, so the river can be paddled year-round without interference by fishing clubs. Steep mountains all around feed many challenging rivers, including the Orchy, which has road access to the most difficult section. There is also the Grand Tully from Stanley to Pencilberg, the classic run for beginners, and a newly built, artificial course called Tside, which will offer reliable water with excellent practice opportunities.

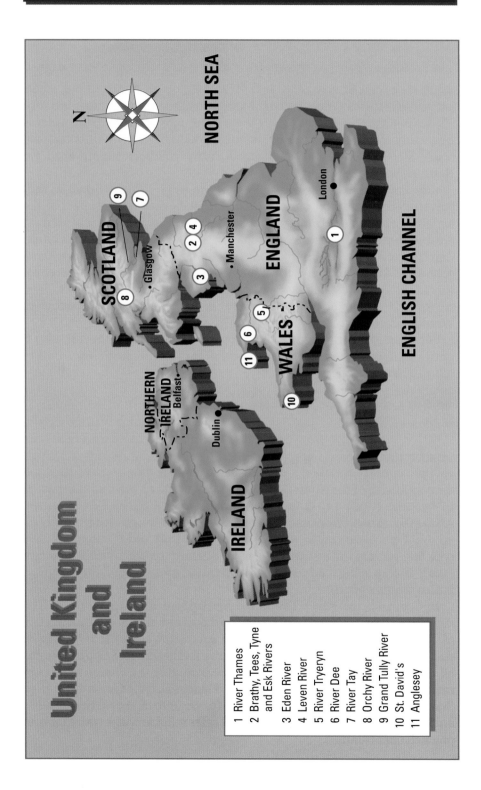

United Kingdom and Ireland

N

NORTH SEA

ENGLISH CHANNEL

SCOTLAND

ENGLAND

WALES

NORTHERN IRELAND

IRELAND

London

Manchester

Glasgow

Belfast

Dublin

1 River Thames
2 Brathy, Tees, Tyne and Esk Rivers
3 Eden River
4 Leven River
5 River Tryeryn
6 River Dee
7 River Tay
8 Orchy River
9 Grand Tully River
10 St. David's
11 Anglesey

Touring clubs for sea kayakers are very active and informative. Contact the British Canoe Union for information (address in appendix). Some of the main centers for sea kayaking include St. David's in southwest Wales and Anglesey in northern Wales. For bigger expeditions, the west coast of Scotland offers many islands and some exciting paddling.

© Windrush Photos/Frank V. Blackburn

Prime sea kayaker's habitat: beautiful cliffs and calm waters in Cardigan Bay, Wales.

Continental Europe

Recreational kayaking is taking off in Europe. For years the sport has had excellent exposure, but participation has been more the domain of competitors and hard-core adventurers. Now nearly every European country has active paddling clubs. Contact the National Governing Body (NGB) of each country for names and addresses of outfitters, clubs, and publications that can help you plan your trip.

Garmisch Partenkirchen, Germany, hosts an English-speaking paddling school open to the public. The local river, the Loisach, is a delightful, narrow, and very technically demanding river, with sections of various difficulties. As with most alpine rivers, the upstream headwaters are pure cascades.

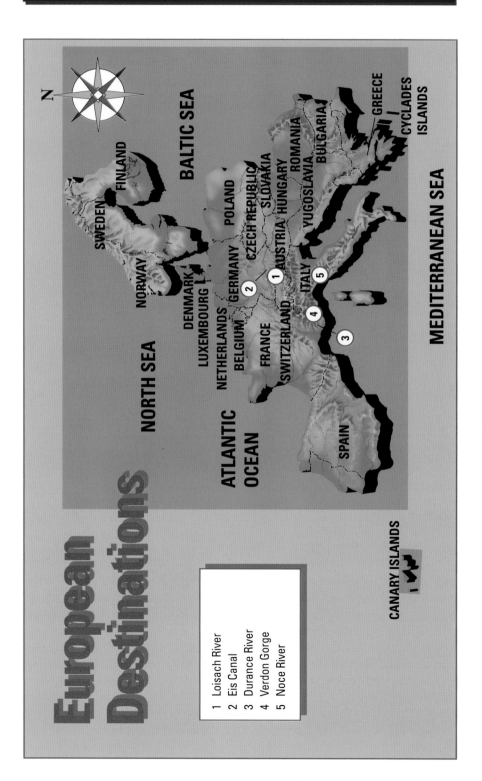

European Destinations

1 Loisach River
2 Eis Canal
3 Durance River
4 Verdon Gorge
5 Noce River

Sea kayakers on the Inn River in southeastern Germany.

Also in Germany, near Augsburg, is the Eis Canal. This is a completely concrete artificial "river," built for the whitewater events of the 1972 Olympics. Two paddling clubs share the facility, so there are many paddlers around to tap for specific information. Frequently you will find the German national team out practicing on the course.

Other rivers in Europe include the Durance, near Embrun, France, and the Verdon Gorge north of the French Riviera. The Noce River is a popular destination in the Italian Alps.

Paddling Down Under

AUSTRALIA

Some of the best wilderness runs are in North Queensland. This is the tropical part of Australia where rivers flow through the World Heritage Rain Forest into the Pacific by the Great Barrier Reef. The Barron, Russell, and Tully rivers offer lots of warm, big-volume Class IV–V whitewater. These rivers are popular for rafting, so you may want to experience them first by raft through one of the Cairns-based rafting companies.

Melbourne is the center of paddling in Australia. The Yarra River flows through the center of Melbourne and is the training site for Australia's kayak team. There are lots of paddling schools here. The Yarra is basically a flatwater river, but in the middle of town the rapid Dyke's Falls has about 300 meters (984 ft) of flowing Class II water. The rapid is natural but has been artificially enhanced for better whitewater paddling. People often paddle there.

The Snowy River in Victoria offers excellent kayak touring in the wilderness. Even with its fairly remote location, it is one of the most commonly paddled rivers in Australia. The run is Class II–III for a 4- to 6-day trip, with nice sandy beaches, excellent camping, and clear water—so clear you can see the bottom.

Tasmania is a long, wet state, so there are lots of short rivers navigable by kayak. One classic is the Mersey River, with safe, bouncy, Class III whitewater. Probably the most famous run in Tasmania is the Franklin River, which is an 8-day wilderness trip on fairly difficult whitewater. The Franklin was saved from damming in the early 1980s by a local environmental movement.

Sea kayaking is very popular around Sydney, because it's on a major, yet very clean, harbor. There's not any whitewater nearby.

The area around the Whitsunday Islands south of Cairns is protected by the Great Barrier Reef, which is about 113 kilometers (70 mi) offshore, so you find fairly calm sea waters, not big waves. These tropical islands are about 11 to 16 kilometers (7–10 mi) apart, making it a really nice place for sea kayaks. Clear water allows an excellent view of the richly colored sealife, and the warm, tropical, sandy conditions are ideal, which has led to the growth of several touring companies in the region.

Adelaide, the capital of South Australia, situated between Perth and Melbourne, is completely flat and therefore a popular area for sea kayaking. Perth has a nice climate (16–27 °C, or 60–80 °F, year-round), warm water, and both sea and whitewater kayaking destinations nearby.

The Katherine Gorge in the Northern Territory is a very popular river trip. Katherine is 323 kilometers (200 mi) south of Darwin, toward the center of

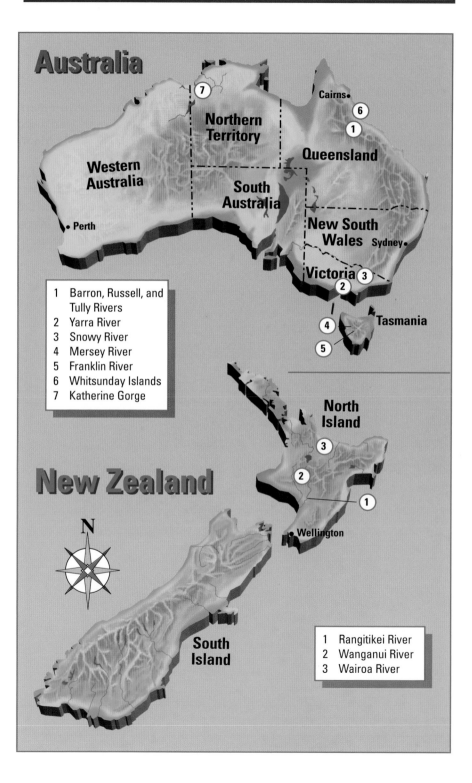

Australia

7

Cairns•

Northern Territory

6

1

Western Australia

Queensland

• Perth

South Australia

New South Wales Sydney•

Victoria 3

2

1 Barron, Russell, and
    Tully Rivers
2 Yarra River
3 Snowy River
4 Mersey River
5 Franklin River
6 Whitsunday Islands
7 Katherine Gorge

4

Tasmania

5

North Island

3

New Zealand

2

1

N

• Wellington

South Island

1 Rangitikei River
2 Wanganui River
3 Wairoa River

Australia. Large liveries on the Katherine River have commercial trips or kayaks for hire.

NEW ZEALAND

The original Polynesian settlers arrived in New Zealand from the northern Pacific by seagoing canoe. Because of the dense forests, canoes were used extensively for transport. Rivers on New Zealand islands have Maori names, such as the Rangitikei, Wanganui, and Wairoa.

The coast of New Zealand is purported to be longer than that of the United States. Much of the coast is exposed and inhospitable, but hundreds of inlets make for wonderful sea kayaking. Most of the fjords on the South Island are unexplored. In addition there are an estimated 2,000 navigable lakes. Sudden changes in weather and extremely cold water present a challenge to paddlers.

© Arndt Schaftlein

Paddling McLaren Falls on the Wairoa River, New Zealand.

The Rest of the World

I am often asked to list my favorite rivers, which is no easy task. It is difficult to pick favorites, and it doesn't seem fair to list the best. As with your friendships, your favorites change. Besides, variety is one reason why exploration is so much fun.

Explore new rivers and coastlines right near where you live! In fact, some of the best waters I have paddled are relatively undiscovered and close to home.

MY FAVORITE RIVERS

To qualify as one of my favorites, a river must have spectacular scenery . . . so spectacular that it threatens to draw my attention away from the excitement of the whitewater. Meanwhile, the whitewater must be intricate, playful, or overpowering, so that it diverts my attention from the scenery. These competing natural dynamics make for a fabulous experience.

In order of distance from my home:

My hometown river (the Animas near Durango, Colorado)

Colorado River, Grand Canyon, Arizona

Chattooga River, South Carolina

Pacuare River, Costa Rica

Verdon River, France

Sjoa River, Norway

Bio-Bio River, Chile

Choru River, Turkey

Varsog River, Tajikistan

7

PURSUING KAYAKING FURTHER

Kayaking offers a world of opportunity. You can kayak to a secret getaway near your home or travel worldwide to exotic locations. As you get further into kayaking, you will discover some interesting varieties of recreational paddling: doing overnight and extended trips, competing, or trying some of the wilder, adrenaline-charging aspects of whitewater like squirt boating or creek boating.

To get the most out of the sport, you will want to have good boat-handling skills and a thoughtful, methodical approach to learning. Whatever your ability, you will have a great time with it.

Fabulous wildlife awaits you. Whether you paddle a sea kayak or a whitewater boat, you can use the boat for easy nature-watching: great blue herons, bald eagles, and foxes are common sights from a boat. Many less common birds and animals can be encountered during even a light paddling trip.

Advanced Whitewater Play

After you've got some experience maneuvering your boat on calm water, you'll probably find you're eager for more challenges. You might try adding some new moves, such as enders, to your repertoire. Enders are the spectacular, air-catching moves of kayaking. Catching air is done by driving your bow upstream into water that is dropping down in steep waves or over ledges, and it requires very precise surfing skills. Most places for enders have a sweet spot with a powerful current to aim the bow. The river's power will propel you up on end.

You might also want to try some different styles of whitewater kayaking that require more specialized boats.

Squirt Boating

Squirt boating is an unusual type of play boating done in tiny kayaks that barely float the paddler. In a squirt boat, a paddler can do cartwheels and even disappear underwater for up to 30 seconds in a maneuver called a mystery move.

Squirt boating requires an extra-small kayak for making extra-special moves.

Creek Boating

Creek boating is an exciting, frightening-looking type of whitewater kayaking. Paddlers frequently run drops and waterfalls in the 10- to 20-foot (3- to 6-m) range. The famed "hair boaters" are pioneering drops of up to 75 feet (23 m) in boats! Needless to say, such trips are for paddlers with excellent skills that are almost always developed first on easy rivers by play boating.

Surf Kayaking

If you have good, reliable surf nearby, this sport might be for you. Surf kayakers ride the ocean waves in boats the way surfers do on surfboards. Surf boats can be quite specialized. The hull design more closely resembles that of whitewater play boats than the touring hull of a sea kayak. Many designs are of the sit-on-top variety for easy exit and easy righting.

Overnight Trips and Expeditions

With a little planning, your kayak can take you to some wonderfully remote places to camp. The boat carries all the weight, but you get the rewards of camping in unusual and rarely visited settings. Sea kayaks are generally much better suited and equipped for overnight and extended trips, but with careful packing, a whitewater kayak can carry adequate gear for several nights out.

Adventure travel companies specializing in kayaking operate trips all over the world. The logistics of arranging an overseas expedition can be as simple as making a few phone calls and faxes.

Competition

Kayak racing is great fun, and paddlers of all levels and ages are getting involved. Through racing, you can learn the basics of training, mental preparation, boat positioning, and paddle placement. These are all fascinating skills, whether you are watching a race or trying to improve your own performance.

Flatwater Sprint Racing

Flatwater sprint racing, at first glance, is very similar to a rowing regatta, but the paddlers are in specialized kayaks and canoes designed for all-out speed in a straight line. Races of 500-, 1,000-, and 10,000-meter distances provide fun competition and an excuse for developing superb technique and fitness. Marathon canoeing events often have kayak classes of competition. Perhaps most famous in the United States is the Finlandia Clean Water Challenge, which is the Tour de France of the paddling world: Athletes race waterways from Chicago to New York City!

Whitewater Slalom Racing

The rules of slalom are simple: Your time from start to finish through 25 gates is measured in seconds. Full-length courses will usually take 200 seconds, while citizen races usually have fewer gates and might take only 90 seconds. You get two race runs on the course, and only the better one counts. If your body, boat, or paddle touches either pole you get a 5-second penalty added to your time. Miss a gate by not getting your head and part of the boat in the gate, and you are assessed a 50-second penalty. The lowest score, including penalty seconds, wins.

The gates must be run in numerical order and in the correct direction. A green striped gate may be negotiated downstream or in the reverse direction, and red gates must be run upstream. Going fast requires being on line, that is, on a fast path calculated to keep you from hitting poles. In every gate of a race course, precision is the key. The fastest paddlers make it look deceptively easy.

Some whitewater paddlers fine-tune their skills by paddling slalom gates instead of by running steeper, more dangerous rivers. Others train and race because nearby rivers and lakes are small, better suited to racing than to recreation. Some people work out or race for the physical and mental challenge. Racing builds your water-reading skills and teaches you to paddle more precisely. Whatever your reason, you'll have a blast doing it.

Plastic cruising boats are perfectly okay to get you started racing. For the most fun and challenge, try a fiberglass racing design for higher performance.

Wildwater Racing

If slalom gates don't excite you, you might want to try the great sport of wildwater racing. In wildwater, the paddlers race for time down 5 miles (8 km) of whitewater. Regional events usually have cruiser classes for recreational boats, or you can try the fast, specialized downriver boat. Wildwater is simpler than slalom to race and train. There are no judges, no penalties, and no courses to hang. Just 20 minutes of river to learn. Wildwater is more adaptable to training on flatwater, and since it is a long aerobic event, it is a great general fitness tool.

Finding Out More

As you start training, you will inevitably have questions about training tips, equipment, and where to find races. The technical side of the canoe and kayak sports is thoroughly covered in a series of books by U.S. Team Coach Bill Endicott. These books and other information are available from the U.S. Canoe and Kayak Team or the American Canoe Association (ACA) offices (see appendix). You will be welcome at local beginners' races. Be forewarned though: Racing is addicting, and you'll find yourself doing more daydreaming. You'll love the exhilaration, camaraderie, competition, and the opportunity to test your skills with gates instead of rocks. I hope you give it a try!

Slalom kayak racing, an Olympic sport.

A Final Reminder

Kayaking has many inherent risks, and simply reading this book won't make you safer. Get some high-quality, on-the-water instruction to ensure that you'll have a good time learning. In just a short time with a good kayak instructor, you can get specific instruction tailored to your skill level.

Think back to the prerequisites to good paddling. Are you comfortable underwater? Are your tummy muscles fighting your hamstrings to get good posture? Notice how flexible the best boaters are. Perhaps a stretching program would improve your enjoyment. Do your strokes stick, rather than pull through the water? In other words, move the boat, not the blade. Can you paddle your boat on edge?

Paddling requires finesse. It helps to be strong, but even the strongest paddler can't overpower the force of the water. Learn to work with the currents and to carefully place your strokes. Lift your line of sight, so you can anticipate instead of react.

Stay relaxed, so you can use optimal amounts of strength and finesse. This,is a young and developing sport with many effective techniques yet to be discovered. So, experiment to find what works best for your strength, balance, and flexibility. But above all, have fun on the water!

You can enjoy the adventure of kayaking.

APPENDIX

Paddling Organizations

U.S. Organizations

American Canoe Association (ACA)
7432 Alban Station Rd., #B226
Springfield, VA 22150
703-451-0141

   River safety, instructor certification.

American Whitewater Affiliation (AWA)
Box 85
Phoenicia, NY 12464
914-688-5569

   Best for hard-core whitewater paddlers on recreation and preserving
   river access. Excellent, homey magazine as well.

Appalachian Mountain Club (AMC)
5 Joy St.
Boston, MA 02108
617-523-0636

> Education and recreation in the Northeast.

U.S. Canoe & Kayak Team (USCKT)
201 S. Capitol Ave., #470
Indianapolis, IN 46225
317-237-5690

> Responsible for preparing the U.S. Olympic and World Championship teams.

Contacts in Other Countries

International Canoe Federation
Dozsa Gyorgy UT 1-3
1143 Budapest
Hungary
36-1-163-4832 phone
36-1-157-5643 fax

Australian Canoe Federation
P.O. Box 666
Glebe 2037, NSW
Australia
61-2-552-4500 phone
61-2-552-4457 fax

Canadian Canoe Association
1600 James Naismith Dr., Suite 709
Gloucester, ON K1B 5N4
Canada
613-748-5623 phone
613-748-5700 fax

British Canoe Union
John Dudderidge House
Adbolton Lane, West Bridgeford
Nottingham, N2G 5AS
Great Britain
44-602-821-1100 phone
44-602-821-797 fax

New Zealand Canoeing Association
P.O. Box 284
6000 Wellington
New Zealand
64-4-357-0584 phone
64-4-359-3287 fax

Association Costaricence de Canoa-Kayak
P.O. Box 472-1200
San Jose
Costa Rica
506-336455 phone
506-554354 fax

Canoes Plus
140 Cotham Rd.
Kew 3101, Victoria
Australia
817-5934

Mobile Adventure
Bridge Works
Knighton Fields Road West
Leicester LE2 6LG
England
0533-83-0659 phone
0533-44-0454 fax

Montbell Kayaks
1-6-17 Itachibort
Nishi-ku Osaka
Japan

Sunday Planning
379-2 Nojiri Shinano-Machi
Kamiminichi-gun
Nagano
Japan
0262-58-2962 fax

Basic Sea Kayaking Books

Sea Kayaking by David Harrison

Written by the editor of *Canoe & Kayak* magazine, this text takes a no-nonsense look at the basics.

The Coastal Kayaking Manual by Randel Washburne

An intermediate textbook.

The Essential Sea Kayaker by David Seidman

Friendly tone and basic information make this the ideal choice for the beginner.

Sea Kayaking by John Dowd

Long considered the bible of the sport.

Derek Hutchinson's Guide to Sea Kayaking

A 25-year veteran of sea kayaking, Hutchinson offers his strong opinions on the sport, along with practical advice on paddling.

Sea Kayaking Videos

Performance Sea Kayaking: The Basics and Beyond
by Kent Ford and John Davis

Entertaining and instructional basics for kayak touring. Stroke technique, trip preparation, and rescues are covered for the beginner. 55 minutes.

What Now? by Maine Sport School

Comprehensive coverage of rescues. 27 minutes.

Kayak Touring by Echomarine Touring Center

Excellent information in a moderate budget production. 28 minutes.

Know Before You Go by TASK (Trade Association of Sea Kayaking)

Introductory information. 10 minutes.

Basic Whitewater Books

Available through most whitewater catalogs and dealers.

Performance Kayaking by former National Champion Steve U'ren
Widely accepted as the bible of the sport.

Whitewater Kayaking Adventure Series by Ray Rowe
Very good coverage of the sport using British terminology.

AMC Handbook by Bruce Lessels
Comprehensive coverage of canoeing and kayaking.

The Bombproof Roll and Beyond by Paul Dutky
Very well-illustrated and -explained look at the concepts behind rolling properly.

ACA Canoeing and Kayaking Instruction Manual by Laurie Gullion
Required text for instructor certification.

River Rescue by Les Bechdel and Slim Ray.
Good coverage of whitewater hazards and accidents.

Whitewater Videos

Available through most whitewater stores and catalogs.

The Kayaker's Edge by Kent Ford and John Davis
Secrets of surfing, sidesurfing, intermediate stroke techniques, rolling, and bracing. "The best general instruction video on the market" —*Outside Magazine*. 58 minutes.

The C-1 Challenge by Kent Ford and John Davis
Fun instructional video with World Champion Kent Ford. Covers advantages of decked canoe paddling, learning to roll, and outfitting for comfort. Hot play scenes and basic stroke instruction. 24 minutes.

Take the Wild Ride by Kent Ford and John Davis
Whitewater rodeo and freestyle kayaking with the world's best play boaters. Very entertaining and instructional. 53 minutes.

Grace Under Pressure by Joe Holt, Kathy Bolyn, and Tom DeCuir

The best rolling video ever produced. Good humor and instruction. 40 minutes.

Heads Up: River Rescue for River Runners by Russ Nichols, Walkabout Productions

A good sampling of the skills necessary for safe times on the river. These other videos by the same producer are excellent as well, but may be available only through the ACA: *Uncalculated Risk, Margin for Error, Whitewater Primer,* and *Cold, Wet and Alive.*

Books on Competition

The following books are by U.S. Team Coach Bill Endicott:

To Win the Worlds. Basic slalom technique.

The Ultimate Run. Elite slalom technique and training.

The River Masters. History of World Championships.

The Danger Zone. Elite downriver technique and training.

The Barton Mold. Olympic sprint Gold Medalist Buck Barton's technique and training.

Videos on Competition

The Citizen Racer Workshop by Kent Ford and John Davis

Basic introduction to racing. Inspiring video footage of World Class racers is explained for racing fans and apprentices. Kayakers and decked canoe paddlers in cruising boats or race boats will enjoy the demonstration of gate technique. Covers basics of training, mental preparation, boat positioning, and paddle placements. 23 minutes

Fast and Clean by Russ Nichols

The very best race season coverage ever. See current top racers (Lugbill, Hearn, and others) as brash juniors 20 years ago. A great inspirational movie for paddlers. 40 minutes.

Stroke Drills by Thierry Humean and Kent Ford

Kayak stroke drills by Dana Chladek (Olympic Bronze Medalist) and Jana Freeburn (U.S. Team member). Canoeing by David Hearn (seven-time World Champion). Set to music with written study guide included. Available from the U.S. Canoe & Kayak Team. 45 minutes.

Whitewater Slalom Judge Training

Learn the rules! Available only from the U.S. Canoe & Kayak Team. 30 minutes.

Periodicals

A good, inexpensive way to learn about new techniques, equipment, outfitters, and destinations.

Canoe & Kayak
P.O. Box 3418
Kirkland, WA 98083
800-692-2663

Paddler
4061 Oceanside Blvd., Ste. M
Oceanside, CA 92056
619-630-2293

Sea Kayaker
P.O. Box 17170
Seattle, WA 98107-7170
206-789-9536

Stores and Mail Order

Cascade Outfitters
P.O. Box 209
145 Pioneer Pkwy.
Springfield, OR 97477
800-223-7238

Colorado Kayak Supply
P.O. Box 3059
22495 Hwy. 285 S.
Buena Vista, CO 81211
800-535-3565

Four Corners Riversports
P.O. Box 379
Durango, CO 81302
800-426-7637
303-259-3893

Great River Outfitters
4180 Elizabeth Lake Rd.
Waterford, MI 48328
810-683-4770

H_2Outfitters
P.O. Box 72
Orrs Island, ME 04066
207-833-5257

Jersey Paddler
1748 Route 88
Brick, NJ 08724

Maximum Whitewater Performance
6211 Ridge Dr.
Bethesda, MD 20816

New Wave Kayak Products
2535 Roundtop Rd.
Middletown, PA 17057
717-944-6320

NOC Mailorder
#41 U.S. 19 W.
Bryson City, NC 28713
704-488-2175

Northwest River Supply
P.O. Box 9186
2009 S. Main
Moscow, ID 83843
800-635-5202
208-883-0811

Outdoor Center of New England
8 Pleasant St.
Millers Falls, MA 01349
413-659-3926

Predator Performance Designs
1652 Duranleau St.
Granville Isle, BC V6H 3S4
Canada
604-688-1928

Wildwater Designs
230 Penllyn Pike
Penllyn, PA 19422
615-646-0157
800-426-2027

Major Kayak Manufacturers

These companies can help you find the closest dealer, as well as provide
information about local demo days, symposia, and so on.

Dagger
P.O. Box 1500
Harriman, TN 37748
615-882-0404

Eddyline
1344 Ashten Rd.
Burlington, WA 98233

Great River Outfitters
3721 Shallow Brook
Bloomfield Hills, MI 48302

Headwaters
P.O. Box 1356
Harriman, TN 37748
615-882-8757

Perception/Aquaterra
P.O. Box 8002
Easley, SC 29640
803-859-7518

Prijon/Wildwasser Sport
P.O. Box 4617
Boulder, CO 80306
303-444-2336

Seda
926 Coolidge Ave.
National City, CA 91950

Wilderness Systems
241 Woodbine St.
High Point, NC 27260

River/Sea Conservation Organizations

Join them and support their efforts!

American Rivers
801 Pennsylvania Ave. SE, Ste. 400
Washington, DC 20003
202-547-6900

The River Network
P.O. Box 8787
Portland, OR 97207-8787
503-241-3506

Trade Association of Sea Kayaking (TASK)
12455 North Wauwatosa Rd.
Mequon, WI 53097
414-242-5228

KAYAKING LINGO

Aleut—Alaskan Eskimo heritage of boat design and techniques.

booties—Neoprene socks or boots for cold-weather comfort.

bow—The front of the boat.

bow rescue (or Eskimo rescue)—The upside-down paddler reaches up to grab the bow of the rescuing boat and uses a hip snap to right the boat. This is a fairly common rescue method used in hazard-free whitewater, where an attentive friend or instructor can help you stay in your boat. In sea kayaking, bow rescues are used only as a practice maneuver, since a sea kayak's limited maneuverability prevents impromptu positioning.

brace—A defensive maneuver done with a paddle blade providing support that can be timed with hip action to keep you right-side up. A brace requires a fair amount of paddle dexterity, so don't be surprised if you actually learn to roll first.

break-in and break-out—British paddlers' terms for "eddy turn" and "peel-out," respectively.

broach—Getting pinned to a rock, either midship or at the ends.

bulkhead—Waterproof partition inside a sea kayak to separate the sitting area from storage and flotation areas in the ends of the boat.

cfs (cubic feet per second)—Measure of water volume in rivers. 100 to 700 cfs is usually considered low volume, and over 3000 cfs is usually considered high volume.

Class I–VI—The whitewater river rating system classifies rivers as Class I to Class VI, from easiest to most difficult. While the system is a useful guide, you need to get a full description of a particular run to get an accurate idea of its difficulty.

creek boating—Creek boating is an exciting, frightening-looking type of whitewater kayaking. Paddlers frequently run drops and waterfalls in the 10- to 20-foot (3- to 6-m) range.

C-to-C roll—The essence of the C-to-C roll is the same as the hip snap. Curve your torso from one side of the kayak to the other to right an upside-down kayak.

deck—The top of the boat that keeps the water out and helps the handling in big waves and swells.

eddy—Quiet spot in whitewater, just downstream of a rock. Paddlers use eddies to stop and rest, to scout an upcoming rapid, and for access to fun play spots.

eddy turn—The foundation move for controlling the speed of your descent down the river. In the quiet of an eddy, you can look at the rest of the rapid, rest, line up for your next move, or get out to portage.

edging—Tilting a kayak by using a J lean.

ender—A spectacular, air-catching move in which the kayak stands straight up on end.

ferry—A maneuver that gets you across the river, from an eddy on one side to an eddy on the other. While this is practical for maneuvering, it can also move you into fun surf waves.

flatwater—Descriptive term for the easiest paddling conditions.

flotation bags—Bags filled with air that fit on either side of the kayak's walls to provide extra flotation in the event of a capsize. Also called float bags.

front—Frontal patterns in the clouds can give immediate feedback on advancing weather, particularly when combined with knowledge about regional weather patterns. Since the sea kayak is the smallest craft on the water, it is the most sensitive to the weather.

glass—Short for fiberglass. Glass boats are built with several layers of fabric woven of fiberglass, Kevlar, or carbon fiber material, impregnated with an epoxy or vinylester resin.

hatch—Storage compartment in a sea kayak with an opening that allows easy access to a lunch cooler or to spare clothes. These airtight and watertight hatches also provide flotation for the boat in event of a swim.

high brace—A good high brace commits your body to the water, with your elbows low, and a minimum of force on your shoulders and blade. Your hands are directly above your elbows.

hip snap—A technique in which the torso and knee motion rights the boat. This helps minimize paddle involvement for good rolls and braces.

hole—A hole is formed by water flowing over a submerged rock. Often used interchangeably with "hydraulic."

hull—The bottom of the boat. The hull design affects the tracking and turning characteristics of the boat.

hydraulic—A hydraulic, like a hole, is formed by water flowing over a submerged rock, although generally less water than forms a hole. The worst hydraulics have evenly formed backwashes with water moving back upstream for 4 feet (1.2 m) or more.

initial stability—Stable platform feel of a boat. Boats that have a lot of initial stability generally have a very hard chine, or sharp corner on the hull.

Inuit—Greenland Eskimo heritage of boat design and technique.

J lean—The J lean, named for the shape of your spine when the lean is done correctly, is a boat tilt with your body weight centered over the boat. This lean keeps most of the weight off your blade so you can use it for balance and for strokes.

keeper—Nastier variation of a hydraulic.

ledge hole—Nastier variation of a hydraulic.

mystery move—A squirt boating maneuver in which the kayak and paddler disappear underwater for up to 30 seconds.

nautical chart—A navigational aid that emphasizes underwater reefs, navigation buoys, and other information not generally found on maps.

offset—Kayak paddle blades are offset: when you lay them on the ground, the blades face in different directions. The offset is usually about 70 degrees.

paddle float—Accessory added to paddle blade, so paddle can be used as an outrigger for reentry stability.

peel-out—A whitewater move done to leave an eddy and head downstream.

poagies—Special gloves for hands and paddle.

pour-over—Nastier variation of a hydraulic.

put-in—Paddlers' jargon for starting point of a trip.

raft and pump—The most common assisted rescue in sea kayaking. Paddlers use the bow-to-stern stabilizing position for reentry and pumping out water.

rocker—The degree to which the hull curves up at the ends. A boat that has a lot of rocker will spin more easily, while a boat that has little rocker will be faster.

safe swimmer's position—Whitewater swimming position: on your back, feet up and pointed downstream, unless the water is less than knee-deep.

sculling—A sculling draw moves you sideways by working the blade back and forth as though spreading peanut butter on the side of your boat. A sculling brace is done for stability, in the motion of spreading icing on the top of the water.

secondary stability—Boats that have solid secondary stability are not quite as stable when you first enter (initial stability), but still have a fair amount of stability when rolled way up on their sides. These boats tend to have a round hull in the cross section.

set-up position—Starting point for an Eskimo roll.

sidesurf—The goal is to sit sideways in a hydraulic, using the wave shape to hold you in position.

spray skirt—One elastic cord of the spray skirt fits around rim and the other around your waist to keep the water out.

squirt boating—Squirt boating is an unusual variety of play boating done in tiny kayaks that barely float the paddler. In a squirt boat, a paddler can do cartwheels, mystery moves, and other tricks.

stern—The rear of the boat.

strainers—Trees or single branches in the river current with water flowing through them that cause a severe pinning hazard.

surfing—Just like surfers on boards in the ocean, kayakers can surf. On rivers the wave stays in the same spot, while on the ocean it moves.

sweep—The primary turning stroke.

sweep roll—Dynamic motion of the paddle near the surface while the boat is being rotated up by hip snap.

swim—Paddlers' jargon describing an unplanned exit from an upside-down kayak.

take-out—Paddlers' jargon for ending point of a trip.

tail wind—Wind coming from behind the paddler. This can often be the hardest wind to maintain directional control in.

tidal current—As the tide rises and falls, large volumes of water are redistributed in the sea. The currents that move this water can be quite strong and can make returning to shore unexpectedly difficult. Tidal changes can have a dramatic effect on the difficulty of paddling. Sometimes a low tide leaves a shallow area exposed, making for a much longer return trip or a nasty slog through mud flats.

torso rotation—The technique of using the powerful torso muscles to power most strokes.

towing—Sea kayak rescue when one paddler simply runs out of energy.

tracking—The ability of the boat to go straight easily.

T rescue—In the T rescue, the rescuer moves perpendicular to the swamped boat and lifts it to empty the water out.

TX rescue—The TX rescue is used when the swamped boat has no bulkhead. This rescue requires pulling the swamped boat far over the deck to drain it completely.

undercut rocks—Undercuts are a water feature where a slab of rock or projecting rock shape forces the current to flow under the rock.

wall—Found inside whitewater boats is a foam pillar that travels the length of the boat, adding stiffness to the deck and flotation to the boat.

wave sets—When ocean waves overlap each other to amplify and offset each other's size. Timing the waves' arrival at the breaking zone can help determine the easiest times for landing and launching.

whitewater—Term describing rapids on a river. Refers to the white, frothing water that kicks off the top of waves.

INDEX

ABOUT THE AUTHOR

Phil DeReimer

Two-time world-champion paddler Kent Ford is a veteran of more than 250 rivers in 23 countries. He has been a member of the U.S. Whitewater Team almost every year since 1977, several times finishing in the top seven in world championships. In 1983 and 1985, he was a member of the world-champion C-1 slalom team, the second team in history to win this title twice.

From 1979 to 1991, Ford was a guide and instructor for Nantahala Outdoor Center in Bryson City, NC. For four of those years, he was the manager of the NOC Instruction Program, the largest canoe/kayak school in the United States.

Ford is the technical producer of several instructional videos, including *Performance Sea Kayaking, The Kayaker's Edge, Solo Playboating!*, and *Take the Wild Ride: Freestyle Kayaking*. He lives in Durango, CO, where he is a self-employed whitewater instructor.

Acknowledgments

I couldn't have finished this project without the help of Maureen Keilty, who bailed me out with extensive last-minute rewriting and proofreading. Maureen served as a pre-editor, helping me rewrite so the editor could understand. Also, thanks to Sandy Bielenberg for proofreading assistance.

Thanks also to my partner in paddlesport instruction, John Davis, for permission to utilize the scripts from *The Kayaker's Edge*, our beginners' kayak instruction video (the best-selling instructional video on kayaking) and from our video *Performance Sea Kayaking: The Basics and Beyond.*

Thanks to Chuck Wales and Amy Wiley for the excellent photography, and to the gang of folks who donated their time and talents as models. Nancy Wiley and the entire crew at Four Corners River Sports in Durango loaned equipment and supplied valuable technical assistance.

A special thanks to Dave Harrison of *Canoe & Kayak* magazine for permission to excerpt portions of technique articles, and to Roy Farrance of Canoes Plus in Australia and Dave Crooks of Mobile Adventure in Britain for technical assistance.

Laurie Gullion, who, as author of *Canoeing* in the Outdoor Pursuits Series, paved the way for another book on paddle sports. I borrowed liberally from her work in areas where the sports overlap.

Holly Gilly, developmental editor for Human Kinetics, proved to be a friendly and efficient editor for this project. Thank you all!